2010 November

The Best
WEDDING RECEPTION...Ever!

The Best WEDDING RECEPTION...*Ever!*

YOUR GUIDE TO CREATING AN UNFORGETTABLY FUN CELEBRATION

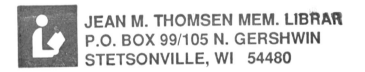
PETER MERRY

SELLERS
PUBLISHING

Published by Sellers Publishing, Inc.

Text copyright © 2010 Peter Merry
All rights reserved.

Sellers Publishing, Inc.
161 John Roberts Road, South Portland, Maine 04106
For ordering information:
(800) 625-3386 toll free
Visit our Web site: www.sellerspublishing.com • E-mail: rsp@rsvp.com

ISBN: 13: 978-1-4162-0606-4
Library of Congress Control Number: 2010925737

10 9 8 7 6 5 4 3 2 1
Printed and bound in China.

Contents

Foreword

What do people most remember about a wedding? Surveys indicate that the most memorable moments occurred at the reception celebration following the wedding ceremony.

That doesn't necessarily mean that the reception is remembered as a great event. Sadly, too often a wedding reception is long-remembered for all the wrong reasons.

In fairness, most engaged couples simply don't have the knowledge or experience that's required to organize an outstanding event. And that's precisely what a wedding reception is — an "event" that requires considerable thought and planning to transform it into a successfully entertaining celebration.

For the past eighteen years, Peter Merry has helped hundreds of couples make the most of their wedding reception. He is an expert on what it takes to create a wedding reception that is fun, entertaining, and truly memorable (for all the right reasons). However, this is not just an opinion based on his credentials. I speak from firsthand knowledge, having been a guest at a reception where he was providing the entertainment. The next best thing to hiring him as your Wedding Entertainment Director is to use this groundbreaking book as an indispensable guide that will help you make the most of your wedding reception celebration.

So here's to your special day. May you and your guests hold cherished memories of your celebration as … "The Best Wedding Reception…Ever!"

Tom Haibeck, Author
Wedding Toasts Made Easy! and *The Wedding MC*
http://www.WeddingToasts.com

Introduction

As the guests arrive for the wedding reception, they can't help but notice how strikingly beautiful the ballroom looks. The floral centerpieces are mounted on golden stands displaying a vivid mixture of pink, lavender, green, and red flower petals. The pale green linens on the tables give the room a feeling of being in a garden setting. The favors feature a lavender ribbon tied in a bow on a small white box with the bride and groom's names and their wedding date in a handwritten font. The cake is set with four tiers and the frosting looks like a heavy, white ribbon that is rolling over the edges. The head table is on a riser with white lights illuminating the tablecloth from underneath the table. The appetizers are displayed with a touch of flair that clearly showcases the passion and creativity of the chef. The lights are slightly dimmed and the music playing in the background is a mixture of vocal jazz artists from the 1940s and 1950s singing songs about love. The catering staff begins to pour champagne as the master of ceremonies tells the 200 guests that the bride and groom and their wedding party are almost ready to make their grand entrance.

Suddenly, the music volume goes up dramatically and the DJ begins to talk as if he's announcing the monster truck show. The wedding party is introduced one couple at a time by just their first names. The best man is named John. He is the groom's father, but unless you are a friend of the groom's family, you wouldn't have known that because the DJ fails to mention it. After the best man's toast, it's time for the bride's father and stepfather to give their formal toasts. The DJ takes the cordless microphone from the best man and walks to the center of the dance floor and introduces these two important men by saying, "Who wants it?" as he holds out the microphone at arm's length. Two men stand up and walk to the dance floor and make formal toasts, but unless you were a friend of the bride's family, you wouldn't know their names, or which one was her father or her stepfather.

During dinner, the music is so loud that the guests have to shout to carry on a conversation. When the meal ends, the guests begin to get restless, but it's a full 20 minutes until the special dances begin. The guests are overheard saying, "When does the fun begin?" The first dance finally starts and when it ends, the DJ announces the father/daughter dance and begins to play the specially selected song as the bride stands on the dance floor waiting for her father to join her. But he's nowhere to be found. "Where's dad?" asks the DJ on the microphone. A few moments later, one of the guests runs out and locates him in the restroom. When the father finally makes it out to the dance floor, the DJ starts their song all over again after making a wisecrack about dad not being ready. When it's time to cut the cake, the DJ invites the guests to gather around. But suddenly there's a commotion as it becomes evident that there is no knife at the cake table. The bride's mother rushes over and tells a catering staff member, who disappears into the kitchen and then comes back with a knife so the bride and groom can finally cut their cake.

When everyone is invited to dance, the DJ tells the guests that they all have to come out to the dance floor if they want the bride and groom to have a long and happy marriage. He then guides them through a series of group dances as the bride and groom begin to shake their heads. It becomes obvious that these were songs that they neither liked nor had requested. There are many times throughout the remainder of the evening when the dance floor is empty. One by one the guests begin to bid the bride and groom farewell. Soon more and more guests are leaving. The bride and groom have the ballroom for another hour, and when the reception is over, they share their last dance with twenty of their closest friends.

The day has ended, they are now married, they had a good time, and their reception was "okay."

As the bride and groom walk down the hallway on the way to their honeymoon suite, they pass a ballroom where another wedding reception has been going on at the same time as theirs. As they pass by, the doors swing open and they see 150 guests dancing, laughing, and enjoying themselves. They overhear a couple saying to each other as they leave the room, "That was the best wedding reception…ever!"

The bride and groom look at each other and begin to wonder what was so different about this reception. "What did they do that we didn't?" they ask themselves.

The truth is there are many different styles of wedding receptions. Some are ordinary while others are creative. Some are traditional while others have a more contemporary feel. Wedding receptions can range from a boring routine to a crazy party. Some seem to drag while others seem to flow smoothly. At many receptions, the bride and groom are the central focus, while at others, guest involvement is encouraged.

What kind of wedding reception do you want? A reception that will capture and hold your guests' attention? The best wedding reception ever?

This book has been written from a unique perspective — one that is focused on the overall entertainment value of your reception. Wedding receptions should be more than just occasions for fancy decorations, beautiful flowers, elegant formalwear, and delicious food. Entertainment is the primary component that will make your wedding reception everything you dreamed it would be. A wedding reception plan that fails to acknowledge the crucial role that the entertainment plays in keeping the guests involved, interested, and enjoying themselves can quickly result in a tedious and mundane experience.

Picture your wedding reception as if it is happening right now. What three words would you choose to describe what you see? Would you be surprised to know that the most common word that comes to mind is "fun"? ("Elegant" and "unique" rounded out the top three.) If you truly want your guests to have fun at your reception, to feel like they are an important part of your celebration instead of just bystanders, then this book is written for you.

You won't find ideas and suggestions related to the decorations, food, dresses, or invitations here. There are more than enough books available on those subjects. Instead, this book gives you creative ideas directly related to ensuring that your guests will have a wonderful time, thanks to the right atmosphere, perfect pacing, and personalized entertainment.

This book gives a wide variety of the most current and creative ideas for making your wedding reception a true reflection of your personality and style. Some of these ideas may seem inappropriate for your plans, while others may leap off the page and connect with your innermost feelings about how you have envisioned your reception. That's to be expected, because we all have different personalities, styles, and tastes. What works for you may not be right for somebody else. But when it comes to creating your wedding reception, there are no more rules. Follow your heart and choose the ideas that inspire you.

This book will also give you clear-cut examples of things that can go wrong, like the real-life examples that were incorporated into the fictional story above, and it will help you increase your chances of preventing them from occurring at your reception. Learning from the mistakes and oversights of others is an important step towards making your reception as flawless as possible.

This book has been divided into three parts, which comprise the three major steps you will need to take to create a truly memorable wedding reception celebration:

PART 1: Beginning Your Production — Choosing the right time, finding the perfect place, and selecting the best qualified cast of players.

PART 2: Creating Your Timeline — Writing a reception plan that will flow smoothly so your guests won't feel bored or restless.

PART 3: Adding Your Personal Style — Putting your fingerprints on every page of your reception plan so the music, guest interactions, and memorable moments will feel like they were created uniquely for you.

As you read through this book, you will notice several pages that spotlight real couples along with their personalized reception agendas. Many of their agendas are quite unique and might give you some ideas for your own reception script.

Feel free to jump ahead to any chapter that features the information you are most interested in or the solutions to issues you are currently trying to resolve.

For additional information on the topics covered in the book, please feel free to visit these Web sites:

TheBestWeddingReceptionEver.com
PeterMerry.com

I sincerely welcome and invite any and all feedback about this book. My e-mail address is: Peter@TheBestWeddingReceptionEver.com.

Peter Merry

PART 1 — *Beginning Your Production*

Choosing the Right Time, Finding the Perfect Place, and Selecting the Best Qualified Cast of Players

Creating a fun, unique, and memorable wedding reception can be very similar to creating a blockbuster movie. Therefore, much of the terminology in this section will be purposely analogous to the art and science of movie-making. Your wedding reception can (and will) be very entertaining, but there is a lot of foundational work to be completed before we can properly set the stage for your opening night premiere. So let's get to work ...

CHAPTER 1

DETERMINING THE TIMING

Choosing the Best Date, Day, and Time for Your Reception

*A*nyone will tell you that the date, day of the week, and time you choose for your wedding and reception will have a major impact on the overall success of your day. Think about the movie industry — there's a good reason why many blockbusters are released in the summer. Kids are known for going to the same hit movie multiple times and so, because school is out, a summer release can lead to increased ticket sales. In this chapter, we will explore the strategic advantages and disadvantages that need to be considered when selecting the date and time for your wedding reception. But no matter what time or what day you choose, the all-important focal point will be that the two of you have finally become husband and wife, and your friends and family will gladly do their part to make it one of the happiest days of your life.

THE SATURDAY EVENING RECEPTION

It's pretty well known that a Saturday evening is the most popular day and time for a wedding reception. Here are a few of the benefits:

- Most of your guests will have the whole day off.

- Your guests will generally have the next day off as well, so they will be more open to staying out later.

- Saturday evening events tend to create a more elegant and relaxed atmosphere.

Here are some issues to consider when choosing a Saturday evening reception:

Make sure that your ceremony does not start too early, so that there won't be a huge gap of time between when your ceremony ends and your reception begins. Many churches, however, have restrictions on how late you can begin

your ceremony on a Saturday. If it can't begin any later than 12:00 p.m., 2:00 p.m., or even 4:00 p.m., but your reception won't be able to begin until 5:00 p.m., 6:00 p.m., or even later, what will your guests do in the meantime? Some suggestions for preparing for this dilemma are given in the section coming up called "How to Bridge the Gap." Scheduling your reception to begin immediately following your ceremony is always your best option.

Many of the best locations and vendors book up their Saturdays 9 months, 18 months, and sometimes even 24 months in advance, especially if the date you are interested in falls into your region's wedding peak season. Peak wedding seasons vary from region to region (often due to seasonal weather patterns such as extreme heat), so be sure to inquire about the peak season in your area. It is especially important to line up your location and most vital vendors before you finalize a Saturday wedding date.

THE SATURDAY AFTERNOON RECEPTION

Saturday afternoon receptions can be an excellent option. They share some of the same benefits as Saturday evenings, but there are some important differences. First, here are some of the additional benefits:

- Lengthy gaps between the ceremony and the reception will not be an issue.

- Some locations and vendors may offer a daytime discount.

- Your guests can enjoy a Saturday evening out on the town after your reception is over.

Here are some issues to consider:

You may not see as many guests dancing because of the "daylight factor." People generally feel more comfortable to let loose and "boogie down" in an evening setting. There's something psychologically freeing about dancing in a darkened room. Good entertainment can compensate for this natural obstacle, and a location that has the ability to block or shut out the sunlight can help as well.

An afternoon time slot may limit the length of your reception. It is very common for popular locations to require that afternoon receptions end by 4:00 or 5:00 p.m., so that they can "turn" their room to prepare for an evening reception. This may have an impact on the entertainment, as your open dancing time may become limited, especially if there have been any other delays (like the ceremony starting late or the photographs running longer than expected).

Because your reception will most likely be over as the evening sets in, some of your guests may be tempted to leave earlier than usual because they have made other plans for their Saturday evening. An early exodus can make a party feel like it's starting to wane, even if the majority of your guests are still dancing or enjoying themselves. If you are mentally prepared for this to occur, however, it won't have much impact on your overall enjoyment.

How to Bridge the Gap

If the gap between your ceremony and your arrival at the reception is an hour or less, appetizers and appropriate background music at a cocktail hour should be more than enough to keep your guests entertained. But if your ceremony and reception are several hours apart, you should seriously consider telling your guests in advance. You could suggest some nearby points of interest, such as a theater, a museum, a historical site, or even a mall, to help your guests fill this gap of time between your ceremony and reception.

THE SUNDAY AFTERNOON
OR EVENING RECEPTION

Sunday afternoon and evening receptions have basically the same benefits and drawbacks as Saturday afternoon and evening receptions, with two major additional benefits:

- Some locations and vendors may be willing to offer substantial Sunday discounts.

- Availability of quality locations and vendors may be much better on Sunday afternoons.

Sunday evening receptions have one major drawback, however. A majority of your guests will probably have to be ready for work on Monday morning, so they may be more inclined to leave earlier in the evening. Try to plan for your reception to wrap up by 9:00 p.m., so your guests can still get home in time to get some sleep. The alternative is to be mentally prepared for an early departure of some of your guests so it won't have much negative impact on your overall enjoyment.

Noting where the majority of your guests have traveled from can help predict the time they'll need to leave. At one of my Sunday evening receptions, the majority of the guests had traveled from a city just over an hour away, so there was a mass exodus around 8:30 p.m. (even though the reception was scheduled to last until 10:00 p.m.). However, if most of the guests have flown in from out of state or out of the country, they will most likely be staying at a nearby hotel and will be less inclined to make an early exit.

THE FRIDAY EVENING RECEPTION

Some of the most common benefits of Friday evening receptions are:

- Your guests will typically have the next day off, so they may be more open to staying out later.

- Friday evening events can still create an elegant and relaxed atmosphere.

- Some locations and vendors may be willing to offer substantial Friday discounts.

- Availability of quality locations and vendors may be much better.

Here are some issues to be considered with Friday evening receptions:

Most of your wedding party and some of your guests may need to take off the whole day, or a half day, from work to participate in or attend your wedding and reception, but it may not always be convenient or possible for them to do so.

Friday evening rush hour traffic can lead to unexpected delays for your wedding party and your guests. Being prepared for this contingency can alleviate any unneeded stress. One option is to provide shuttle buses or a limo service for your wedding party members and/or your immediate family. The rush hour traffic may even cause delays for your vendors, so you might want to make sure that they intend to arrive earlier than normal.

After working a half day or even all day, some of your guests may feel a little worn out when it is finally time to open up the dance floor. Instead of "cutting a rug," some of them may choose to cut out earlier than you had expected. But if you are mentally prepared for this to occur, it shouldn't have much impact on your overall enjoyment.

THE WEEKDAY EVENING RECEPTION

If you are considering a weekday evening reception, you will find a mixture of the benefits and drawbacks from the Friday evening reception and Sunday evening reception options. Here are some of the most common benefits:

- Some locations and vendors may be willing to offer substantial weekday discounts.

- Availability of quality locations and vendors may be much better on weekday evenings.

Here are some possible drawbacks of a weekday evening reception:

Your guests may need to take the day off, or half the day off, from their jobs in order to attend. Your guests may be inclined to leave earlier than you desired, especially if they had to work a full or half day before attending your reception or if they have to work the next day. Weekday evening rush hour traffic may cause unexpected delays for your wedding party, your guests, and even your vendors.

BENEFITS VS. DRAWBACKS

This chart can be used to help you identify the issues that are most important to you when determining which day and time might work best for your celebration.

	Saturday Afternoon	Saturday Evening	Sunday Afternoon	Sunday Evening	Friday Evening	Weekday Evening
GUEST ISSUES:						
Guests will have the whole day off from work	✓	✓	✓	✓		
Guests may need to take the day off from work					✓	✓
Guests may need to work for all or part of the day					✓	✓
Guests will have the following day off from work	✓	✓			✓	
Guests will have a full workday the following day			✓	✓		✓
Guests will have their evening free for themselves	✓		✓			
Guests may get delayed in rush hour traffic					✓	✓
Guests will be more inclined to dance in the evening		✓		✓	✓	✓
Guests will be less inclined to dance in the daylight	✓		✓			
Guests may be more inclined to stay longer		✓				
Guests may be more inclined to leave early	✓		✓	✓	✓	✓
TIMING ISSUES:						
Possible lengthy gap between ceremony and reception		✓		✓	✓	
No issue with a gap between the ceremony and reception	✓		✓			✓
Possible restrictions on your ending time	✓		✓			
Unforeseen delays could limit time for dancing	✓		✓			
LOCATION/VENDOR ISSUES:						
May have less short-term availability	✓	✓				
May have more short-term availability			✓	✓	✓	✓
May have less local "peak season" availability	✓	✓				
May have more local "peak season" availability			✓	✓	✓	✓

Holidays can provide an added benefit to particular days that might not otherwise have been as attractive. Here are some examples:

Memorial Day and Labor Day always occur on Mondays, thus enabling the Sunday evenings that precede them to share the same benefits that Saturday evenings normally have. The afternoons or evenings of Memorial Day and Labor Day can also be beneficial choices, as they will share the same benefits of a Sunday afternoon or evening reception. But these three-day holiday weekends are also popular times for short trips, so you may need to send out your invitations a little earlier than normal, or at least send out "save the date" cards.

The 4th of July can create a three-day weekend. This can allow a Thursday evening reception to share the same benefits as a Friday evening reception. On the same note, a Sunday evening reception can adopt the benefits of a Saturday evening reception. If the 4th of July occurs midweek, the evening of July 3rd can have the same feel as a Friday evening reception. The 4th of July can also be a good day for a wedding reception, especially if you are located near a large fireworks display and would like a patriotic theme. And of course, you can always joke with your friends that you picked that date to make sure there are fireworks on your wedding night!

Thanksgiving always occurs on a Thursday and is generally a holiday that brings families together, even from long distances. Thanksgiving typically creates a four-day weekend, which can give the Friday that follows it the same benefits of a typical Saturday. One added benefit of a Thanksgiving weekend wedding is that you can save your extended family the expense of making another trip at a different time for your wedding.

New Year's Eve and New Year's Day offer their own advantages as well. Just like the 4th of July, New Year's Day can create a three-day weekend or give a weekday added benefits. But the other advantage includes the state of mind that your guests are in

Holidays to Keep in Mind

Memorial Day: Last Monday in May

Labor Day: First Monday in September

Independence Day: July 4th (can create a 3-day weekend)

Thanksgiving Day: Fourth Thursday in November (creates a 4-day weekend)

New Year's Eve & New Year's Day: December 31st & January 1st (can create a 3-day weekend)

when celebrating the New Year. They will not only be happy and ready to celebrate your new commitment to each other, but they'll also be in a party mood. However, some locations and vendors may not only have limited availability, but they may also require a premium fee. New Year's Eve is a popular night with a lot of demand, so don't be surprised if you need to exceed your initial budget expectations.

One possible drawback about a holiday wedding is that your friends and family may not want to give up their entire holiday weekend.

THE IMPACT OF LARGE SPORTING EVENTS

Large sporting events can also have an impact on the date you choose for your wedding reception. Here are some examples:

In 2002, Game 7 of the Los Angeles Lakers semifinal competition against the Sacramento Kings for the NBA Championship title was considered by many to be the best game of the whole championship series. That game drew more attention that day than anything else in all of Southern California. During the dinner of my clients' reception, guests congregated outside around small portable radios and mini-televisions in an attempt to follow the game. I approached my clients with a few options, and they wisely opted to have me announce game updates throughout the meal, which I prompted by playing the theme music from ESPN's SportsCenter. By doing this, we kept a larger portion of the guests inside for the special dances, and when the Lakers finally won, it was just as we were beginning the open dancing. The guests were so enthusiastic, their energy spilled right over to the dance floor.

That same year, when the Anaheim Angels made it into the World Series for the

Large Sporting Events

Pro Football
Playoffs January
Super Bowl Last Sunday in January or first Sunday in February

Pro Basketball
Playoffs Mid-April through May
Finals Early to Mid-June

Pro Baseball
Playoffs Early to mid-October
World Series Late October

Pro Hockey
Playoffs Mid April to late May
Stanley Cup Late May or early June

College Football
Bowl Games
Mid-December to early January

College Basketball
Final Four Playoffs Mid-March to early April

first time in the history of their franchise, all of Orange County instantly became "diehard" baseball fans. I entertained at three weddings that were impacted by the World Series. Two of them dealt with it smoothly, while one didn't fare quite as well.

The bride and groom of the first two receptions asked me to give regular updates of the score, and when the news was good, I was more than happy to do so. In the reception that took a turn for the worse, my clients allowed a guest to bring in a small television, and pretty soon, the guests were more focused on that little TV than on the real reason why they had come together.

The point is that outside events can take a priority in the minds of your guests and, unless these circumstances are handled wisely, they can take over your reception in a detrimental way. So take some time to investigate whether any large sporting events (or other large-scale events) might coincide with your prospective dates.

It should also be noted that a large sporting event near your reception location can cause traffic delays and hotel room shortages for your out-of-town guests. According to Jim Cerone, a Wedding Entertainment Director based in Indianapolis, "Nobody plans a wedding reception in Indianapolis on Memorial Day weekend because of the Indy 500 race. This annual formula racing championship is attended by over 650,000 fans and there are never any local hotel rooms available over that weekend."

PETE & JUDY

APRIL 5, 2009
WILLIAMSBURG, VIRGINIA

Fife & Drum Parade to the Reception

Pete and Judy were married in Historic Colonial Williamsburg. Their ceremony took place in an outdoor, garden setting that was across the street from their reception location. Wanting to create a transition from their cocktail hour to their reception that was both memorable and fitting, they asked the local Fife & Drum Corps to lead them and all of their guests in a parade from the garden area to the ballroom.

*VOCAL PERFORMANCE

Pete and Judy were big fans of Broadway musical theatre. Having an extensive background in musical theater herself, Elisabeth Scott Daley, their Wedding Entertainment Director, was able to perform one of their favorite songs from "Phantom of the Opera" during the meal for them.

RECEPTION AGENDA

4:30–5:30
Drinks & Appetizers
"The Imperial March"
by John Williams

5:40
Grand Entrance
"The Imperial March"
by John Williams

5:50
First Dance
"The First Man You Remember"
by Michael Crawford

5:55
**Father/Daughter-
Mother/Son Dance**
"There You'll Be" by Faith Hill

6:00–7:15
Dinner

6:35
* Vocal Performance
"All I Ask Of You"
by Elisabeth Scott Daley

7:15–7:45
Open Dancing

7:45
Toasts

8:00
Cake Cutting
"The Way You Do The Things You Do"
by UB40

8:10
Garter & Bouquet Toss
"Tootsie Roll" by 69 Boyz
"I'm Too Sexy" by Right Said Fred
"Soul Bossa Nova" by Quincy Jones
"Gettin' Jiggy Wit It" by Will Smith
"Single Ladies (Put A Ring On It)"
by Beyoncé
"(You Drive Me) Crazy"
by Britney Spears

8:20–9:45
Open Dancing

9:45
Last Dance
"Somewhere Over The Rainbow/
What A Wonderful World"
by Israel Kamakawiwo'ole

When scheduling your wedding reception, it is important to decide how long your celebration should last. If your reception is too short, the time for dancing may get squeezed to a minimum and some of your events may feel rushed. If you schedule too much time, your guests may leave earlier than you might have preferred.

Four hours is the minimum length of time I would suggest for a reception (ceremony not included), as it will give you just enough time to enjoy a meal, take care of all the traditional events you have scheduled, and still have a good hour or more of open dancing. Six hours is a suggested maximum, as your guests will have been celebrating with you since your ceremony began. Keeping the party going too long will be a problem only if you are planning to have a big sendoff or if you want the majority of your guests to be involved all the way to the end of your reception. If your plan includes dancing late into the night with a core group of friends (after most of the guests have already gone home), then preparing for a reception to last six hours or more might not be unreasonable. The longest weddings I have been involved with lasted a total of eight hours, including the ceremony and cocktail hour.

You might also want to examine the local norms for your region. In some parts of Canada, the reception alone can last eight hours with guests dancing for three to four hours, or more, after the traditional festivities have been completed. In Hawaii, many wedding receptions are three hours or less. If you are unsure about your region's norms, ask some of your local vendors.

The real question is, what kind of an ending do you want your guests to remember? Comparing your wedding reception to a blockbuster movie, think back on how many movies you have seen that kept your attention and interest all the way through, but then ended poorly. No matter how good the rest of the movie was, you will always remember its weak ending. In the same way, your wedding reception can have a strong ending or an ending that trails off. Neither option is right or wrong. The only thing that matters is what kind of ending best fits your style. If your style is best reflected in a party that goes all night long, then by all means, schedule your reception to continue until midnight or later. But if your primary concern is that the majority of your guests will see you off as you leave for your honeymoon, you might want to prepare to end at a high point, leaving your guests wanting just a little bit more. This type of ending can have a positive lasting impact with your guests — one that you will be hearing about for years to come.

It is important to plan the bride and groom's exit in advance, because when you are in the moment, you may feel inclined to "get your money's worth" from your

location and/or your entertainment by going until 11:00 p.m. as you had contracted, when a 10:00 p.m. ending might result in a stronger and more memorable finale. In the long run, if creating a memorable ending is your priority, you will still get your money's worth by choosing to wrap things up at 10:00 p.m., and your guests will still have an hour to say their goodbyes before the room has to be cleared.

Randy Bartlett, a nationally known DJ trainer and Wedding Entertainment Director based out of Sacramento, California, suggests yet another option for ending your celebration. "You can have the best of both worlds by staging an 'early ending' with a finale song (including a send-off if you'd like) and then announcing the beginning of 'the after party' where the music can be geared more towards the younger guests who will be more likely to stay later into the night. This will give the older guests, who might be inclined to leave early, the feeling that they have participated in the entire reception. And it can also create a more memorable ending for the majority of your guests while still allowing you to extend the dancing late into the night."

CHAPTER 2

PRIORITIZING THE ENTERTAINMENT IN YOUR BUDGET

Examining the Value of an Entertaining Celebration

. . . .

*J*ust a few hours before the ceremony was to begin at one of my weddings several years ago, the location staff realized the flowers hadn't arrived. They frantically made phone calls, while word began circulating that this particular florist had recently started pulling "no shows" due to an alleged drug habit. Finally, the location staff went out to buy floral arrangements from a nearby grocery store. The flowers were decidedly minimal and didn't match the theme and colors the bride had chosen for her day. However, when the night ended, most of the guests were still in attendance, dancing with the bride and groom. Guests then lined up outside to blow bubbles and give them a fun sendoff. Not a single guest was overheard saying, "It's too bad their flowers didn't show up. Their wedding would have been a lot more fun."

I started to wonder what might have happened if I hadn't shown up to provide the music and entertainment for the reception. What if the location staff had been able to find music on an iPod to play over the in-house speakers, but it didn't include the songs the bride and groom had selected for their special moments, like their first dance? What if most of their guests had departed early and only a handful of people were left to blow bubbles as they made their exit? What if their reception ended up lacking any memorable moments filled with laughter or dancing?

Try to picture your reception with certain key components removed. It can become quite clear which of those components will play the most important roles in making your celebration one that will be enjoyed and remembered for a long time.

. . . .

WHAT ARE YOUR PRIORITIES?

Establishing your priorities in advance will help you plan your wedding budget. The big question to ask yourself is, "What facets of my wedding reception are most important to me?"

If your answer is the photographs, you might want to set aside a larger portion of your budget for securing a photographer whose style and experience will be a perfect match for your desires. This priority will likely influence your choices of decorations, flowers, and apparel, so that your photos will truly look their best. But don't overlook the impact that the entertainment will have by helping to create the fun, memorable moments that your photographer will be trying to capture.

If you say that the food would be the most important component of your reception, you will most likely select your location based on the type and quality of food served there. You might then have less to spend on entertainment, so your guests may not linger much past the end of the meal. But at least when your guests do leave, they will have enjoyed a truly memorable meal.

If you find yourself compelled to make the decorations the cornerstone of your reception, you might need to find a designer who can turn your vision into reality. When your guests first walk into the setting you have created for them, they may find themselves gasping in awe. But when the meal is over and they have become accustomed to the décor, what will keep them from becoming bored?

If keeping your guests involved and entertained is your highest priority, here are some facts you should consider before determining how much you can afford to invest in quality, personalized entertainment.

THE ROLE OF ENTERTAINMENT

Ask yourself, "How big a role will the quality of the entertainment play in the overall success of my reception?"

In post-reception surveys tabulated by DJs who are members of DiscJockeyAmerica.com (an online forum where professional Mobile DJs from around the world share ideas for creating better performances and improving their services), clients who

made entertainment a high priority for their receptions answered the above question by stating that the quality of their entertainment was 80 percent (or more) responsible for the success of their receptions.

For years, many have said, "The music makes or breaks the reception." But the truth is that music is just one part of the overall services provided by professional wedding entertainment vendors to ensure a great reception — one that is continuously entertaining for all of your guests. The statement that would ring more true is: "The entertainment makes or breaks the reception."

It's eye-opening to note that the popular wedding magazines, books, and television shows will never give you advice on how to hire "film," because wedding photographers are already recognized as professionals and artists with unique talents, skills, and personal styles. Yet those same bridal information resources are constantly offering tips on how to hire "music" for your reception. Like "film" to a photographer, "music" is a tool and only a part of the whole suite of services that professional wedding entertainers regularly provide. If "music" were all that you needed to create an entertaining reception, the result would simply be an extended cocktail hour.

This is what good-quality wedding entertainment should be:

- The entertainment at a wedding (whether you choose a DJ or a band) also typically serves as the master of ceremonies by announcing the formalities in an appropriate manner.

- The entertainment will help you plan the agenda to ensure the proper pacing needed to prevent your guests from becoming bored.

- The entertainment should communicate with you, your parents, your wedding party members, and the other vendors behind the scenes in an ongoing manner, keeping your reception agenda on track and flowing smoothly.

- The entertainment should brainstorm in advance with you to develop personalized moments that will leave your guests with lasting memories of your unforgettable celebration.

Quality entertainment requires professionalism, artistry, and unique talent and skill. Don't be fooled into thinking that someone who will "just push play" on a CD deck, playing the same set of songs they play every week, can make your reception fun and entertaining. I will discuss these issues in greater detail in Chapter 6: "Auditioning for Talent."

SOME FOOD FOR THOUGHT

In July 2003, *St. Louis Bride & Groom Magazine* surveyed brides within weeks of their wedding. They were asked what they wished they had done differently when creating their budgets and hiring their vendors. Seventy-eight percent said they wished they had given top priority to their decisions about entertainment, and 72 percent wished they had spent more time researching before selecting their entertainment. That's a pretty high percentage of wedding clients who appear to be looking back at their recent entertainment decisions with buyer's remorse.

Nearly 100 percent of them said that, in retrospect, they would have gladly set aside more money from their budget in an effort to have a better quality of entertainment. This may be the result of the current budget suggestions in bridal magazines and popular bridal books that recommend setting aside only 5 to 10 percent of your total budget for the purpose of securing "music." But as I said earlier, music cannot create a successful reception all by itself. Overall, entertainment service is what really sets the tone, keeps the agenda flowing smoothly, and maintains the ongoing interest of the guests.

Therefore, it is my suggestion and conviction that spending more to secure the quality of entertainment that you desire for your reception is an investment in its overall success. How much is the success of your reception really worth? Is 15 percent of your total budget a fair amount? Twenty percent? How about 25 percent?

In seminars and articles he has produced for the mobile DJ industry, Mark Ferrell has repeatedly said, "The amount a person spends on entertainment is directly proportional to the quality of entertainment they will receive, which is directly proportional to the overall success of their reception." When movie producers want to make a successful comedy, they have been known to invest up to $25 million to secure Jim Carrey as the lead actor. They recognize that Jim Carrey's track record and fan base ensure a film that will make at least $100 million, if not more, in return.

How different is the entertainment you will select for your reception? Sure, your definition of a successful reception is much different than the definition of success for a blockbuster movie, but the responsibility that Jim Carrey will have in helping to make the movie successful is very similar to the responsibility of your entertainment to ensure that your reception will be a success.

BUDGETARY THOUGHTS

If an entertaining reception is of the highest priority to you, keep in mind that there are many different aspects of your overall budget that can be easily trimmed without impacting the overall entertainment value of your reception in any way. I have seen wedding clients spend hundreds of dollars on favors (most of which get discarded), over a thousand dollars on chair covers, and tens of thousands on flowers. If you have attended any receptions lately, think about them. Were they fun? Enjoyable? Were they entertaining or were they boring? The most lavish of weddings can still be disappointing if the guests are bored or restless and the entertainment is not doing a good job of entertaining. On the other hand, a low-budget reception with lovely (but less-than-lavish) flowers, no chair covers or favors, and a simple meal, can still be an incredibly memorable reception if the value of the entertainment is given a high priority.

PETER & NICOLE

JULY 30, 2005
MALIBU, CALIFORNIA

Let Them Eat . . . Double Doubles!

Peter and Nichole wanted to surprise their guests with something different for dinner. So after the salads had been served, the guests were invited to guess what was going to be served for the entrée. Right on cue, the staff from In & Out Burger (a popular Southern California burger chain) came strolling out in their white uniforms with their red aprons and paper hats while the In & Out Burger jingle was playing. The guests began to cheer! Not only did they save a bundle on their food budget, Peter and Nichole also got to enjoy their favorite meal on their wedding day.

* FATHER/DAUGHTER & MOTHER/SON DANCE

Peter and Nichole prerecorded special surprise messages for her father and for his mother, which were then mixed into the father/daughter and mother/son dance songs.

RECEPTION AGENDA

5:50–6:50
Drinks & Appetizers

6:50
Grand Entrance
"You Really Got Me"
by Van Halen

7:00
First Dance
"Better Together"
by Jack Johnson

7:05
Toasts

7:15–8:15
Dinner

8:15
* Father/Daughter Dance
"Isn't She Lovely"
by Stevie Wonder

8:20
* Mother/Son Dance
"In My Life"
by The Beatles

8:25–10:00
Open Dancing

10:00
Cake Cutting
"When I'm Sixty-Four"
by The Beatles
"Satisfaction"
by The Rolling Stones

10:15
Bouquet & Garter Toss
"Naughty Girl" by Beyoncé
"Hollaback Girl" by Gwen Stefani
"Love Machine" by The Miracles
"Lady" by Lenny Kravitz
"Come Out and Play"
by The Offspring

10:25–12:30 (a.m.)
Open Dancing

12:30 (a.m.)
Last Dance
"It Ain't Over 'Til It's Over"
by Lenny Kravitz

A WINNING STRATEGY

Based on my almost two decades of involvement in the wedding industry, it is my opinion that the top three components of a successful reception are the location, the photographer, and the entertainment. Finding a location that will fulfill your expectations, create great backdrops for your photos, and allow for a quality entertainment experience is crucial. Finding a photographer who can capture your memories with the style and quality you desire is vital. Finding entertainment that can work with your location and your photographer to create a smooth-flowing reception with memorable moments and personalized touches will be invaluable. So do your research and select the best that you can find in all three categories. Then survey the remaining funds in your total budget and begin working a strict budget from there.

Whether your budget is under $10,000 or upwards of $60,000 or more, your priorities will determine what you can and can't afford, and where you should or shouldn't be spending more than you had originally planned. Write a list of your priorities, and if hosting an entertaining reception is a high priority, then it is my hope that the information contained in the next few chapters will help you select the best vendors and get the best value for your budget.

CHAPTER 3
PONDERING THE RESPONSIBILITIES OF THE PRODUCER

Deciding Who Will Be Your Lead Producer

. . . .

*P*lanning a wedding can be a stress-filled task that may often feel overwhelming. Trying to do it all by yourself can often lead to increased pressure, which may very well make you and those you are closest to feel miserable instead of ecstatic about your fast approaching wedding day. So how do you determine how much help you will really need? Is a professional coordinator always the best option? Could enlisting the services of a family friend be all you need?

. . . .

WHAT IS THE ROLE OF A PRODUCER?

A producer in the movie industry has several important responsibilities. First and foremost, the producer is the movie's financial backer. As the primary investor, the producer has strong input concerning who will be the director, the lead actors, the set and costume designers, and he or she also influences the locations for filming, the release date and, of course, the budget.

You and your immediate family (if they are helping to finance your wedding) are the producers of your wedding day. Just as some independent films are produced on a shoestring budget by the director, who may also be the lead actor and screenwriter, a small-scale wedding on a tight budget might be just fine as a do-it-yourself production. But when Hollywood wants to create a summer blockbuster with a budget of $100 million, a producer who has already produced well-known hit movies is sought. In the same way, a professional coordinator who has already produced hundreds of successful weddings will not only help relieve stress and anxiety, but he will also know the best options in locations, vendors, and decorations to fit within your budget and still fulfill your desires.

Keep in mind that most producers are not directors. The role of the director is to examine the script and rewrite certain scenes, if needed. The director will inform the actors about how to best fulfill their roles—not only how to act as their characters, but also where they will need to stand and walk and sit for each and every shot. The director will control the lighting and the pacing of the action. The director will select the music that will create the best soundtrack for the film. The producer and director fulfill two very different roles. I will discuss these issues in greater detail in Chapter 7: "Nominating the Best Director."

THE DO-IT-YOURSELF PRODUCTION

As I mentioned earlier, you are already the producer of your wedding day. But if you are planning to manage all of the producer responsibilities by yourself, here are some things you might want to consider:

How much time will it take?

Producing a wedding will take much longer than you might expect. Most weddings take anywhere from nine months to a year or more to produce. Many weekends and weeknights will be sacrificed for location visits, vendor meetings, dress fittings, picking out rings, trying on tuxes, and selecting floral arrangements, not to mention bridal showers, engagement parties, and bachelor/bachelorette parties. Examine how much of your own time you can afford to invest in your production. If you have the free time to manage these details, then a do-it-yourself production may be achievable.

How much help will you really need?

Do you already have a pretty strong game plan or are you at a loss for where to begin? Do you already have your location picked out, along with several of your key vendors? Do you have a clear idea of the type of decorations and flowers you want and where to get them? Have you already found your dress and selected what your wedding party will wear? Then perhaps you can handle the other producer details on your own. But if you find yourself feeling overwhelmed after just leafing through a bridal magazine, you might want to consider hiring a professional coordinator.

Who will manage the production details on your wedding day?

Who will make sure your placecards for the reception seating arrangements are in their proper places? Who will look after your favors and make sure your centerpieces are set the way you wanted? Who will make sure the flowers from the ceremony are safely transported to your reception? Who will make sure that your clothes are put where they need to be for your departure? Who will properly secure and/or transport your wedding gifts from the reception?

These and many other production details need to be covered on your wedding day. If you've already decided who will take care of them, good for you! But if not, this is where a professional coordinator can help. Or, at the very least, you might want to hire a "day of the wedding" coordinator.

ENLISTING A FAMILY MEMBER OR FRIEND

Working with a family member or friend as your wedding producer may be like working with a diamond in the rough or taking a trip down a rocky road. Here are some points to consider:

Does he have any wedding production experience?

Did he recently get married, so he has that experience to share? Did he help produce the weddings of other relatives or friends? How well did he do? Don't be afraid to ask for references or a portfolio of pictures and ideas. If he is trying to start a wedding coordination service, will he be learning from his mistakes during your reception?

You get what you pay for.

If your friend or relative is managing your production responsibilities as a favor, will he revert to saying, "It's not like I'm being paid," if something goes wrong? It is essential to clearly define, in advance, your expectations, as well as the roles and responsibilities of your producer. If the producer is being paid for his services, make sure it is a fair and reasonable amount. If he is serving as a volunteer, say thanks by arranging for a generous gratuity, a hotel suite for two, or something else that would be meaningful.

Can your relationship withstand the pressure?

Is this person someone you would feel comfortable saying "no" to? Would your relationship be harmed if things go awry? Are you completely confident that this person will effectively manage his duties? If you feel any hesitation when answering these questions, a professional coordinator may be the best option. Better to retain your friendship and maintain your sanity than to lose both in the tumultuous events that can unfold during a wedding production.

THE PROFESSIONAL WEDDING COORDINATOR

If you decide you need a professional to help with the production of your wedding day, selecting the right person will have a dramatic impact on its overall success. A professional wedding coordinator will help turn your visions into reality while also helping you to select vendors for your winning team. However, finding the right person for the job can be a challenge. Here are some things to consider as you interview different wedding coordinators:

How much wedding production experience does he have?

A professional wedding coordinator should have a portfolio of client references, unique wedding ideas, and preferred vendors. Do your research, call his references, and talk to the vendors he recommends. Keep in mind that some wedding professionals may have many years of experience but tend to do the same kind of weddings over and over again year after year. Look for diversity in the type and style of weddings that he has produced.

Finding a Proven Professional Coordinator

If you are looking for a professional coordinator who has proven skills, training, and expertise in his field, do a search among the members of the ABC (Association of Bridal Consultants) in your area. The ABC is the longest-running association for consultants in the United States. It offers advanced training and certifies its members with the titles of Professional Bridal Consultant, Accredited Bridal Consultant, and Master Bridal Consultant. Members are listed on the official ABC Web site (http://www.BridalAssn.com).

Unlike the ABC certification process, which is based on experience and con-tinuing education, The Wedding Planning Institute (http://www.WeddingPlanningInstitute.com) offers a certification process based on a forty-hour college curriculum that takes eleven weeks to complete. Students must assist at a wedding during the course as well as pass a series of tests and a final certification test.

There are other courses and organizations that offer similar services and lists of professional coordinators, but the two organizations noted above are currently the most prominent.

Is this a person I can work with?

Wedding coordinators provide different types of services. Some will manage all of the details while seeking your input on all the available options. Others will give you a few choices while making many of the style choices themselves. Neither approach is right or wrong. They just cater to different types of clients. Once you have decided how involved you want to be, then the type of coordinator who will best fit your needs should become apparent. Remember, this is a person you will be working with very closely over several months. Finding a personality match should be an important part of the decision.

What is your coordinator's policy regarding a preferred vendors list?

Professional coordinators will refer and recommend the best quality vendors they can find within your budget range because they recognize that truly professional vendors make them look even more professional in return. However, some coordinators may make a referral based on a referral fee they receive from vendors. This practice, although somewhat common, may not serve your best interests. Don't be afraid to ask pointed questions about this apparent conflict of interest before selecting your coordinator.

Will your coordinator work as a team player with your other vendors?

A team player recognizes that constant and mutually respectful communication is an important ingredient in accomplishing a successful wedding reception. How soon will your coordinator contact the other vendors you have already selected? Will it be the week of the wedding, or right after he has been hired? Advance contact from the coordinator gives your other vendors confidence that your production details are in good hands. A coordinator who waits until the week of the wedding to make first contact with your other vendors may cause unneeded stress and anxiety for your vendors and for you, as they may have questions and issues that are hard to answer or resolve with less than a week to go. Ask the coordinator about challenges he has faced with other vendors and what he did to resolve them. Professional coordinators have worked with some of the best and some of the worst wedding vendors around, and they have undoubtedly encountered tense and trying situations. Pay close attention to the coordinator's answers and look for strategies he has developed for preventing future stressful situations. If no strategies have been developed, then he may be placing the blame elsewhere instead of actively seeking solutions.

Will the coordinator allow the entertainment vendors to give input regarding the reception agenda?

A professional coordinator will value the input provided by your entertainment vendors regarding the room layout, the reception agenda, and the music selections. If the coordinator is unwilling to meet with or work with your entertainment vendors in advance, then you might be allowing a producer, who possibly has little or no entertainment experience, to create an agenda that might not be very entertaining. Your coordinator will trust the florist to give input on the floral arrangements; he should be just as open to creative input from your entertainment vendors.

What preparations does the coordinator make for emergencies?

A professional coordinator is prepared for just about everything. Wedding coordinators commonly carry an emergency kit filled with buttons, needles, thread, candles, lighters, matches, shoe polish, makeup, antacids, and other items that in the heat of the moment can turn a near-disaster into a heroic save. Ask your coordinator about the preparations he has made to prevent problems (or to resolve them, should they occur). Ask to see a checklist of the details that the coordinator would manage to prevent those details from being overlooked. Ask about his emergency kit, or about the last fiasco (or near fiasco) that he encountered and how it was effectively resolved.

CHAPTER 4

SCOUTING FOR THE PERFECT LOCATION
Finding the Right Venue for Your Reception

. . . .

*T*he location you choose for your reception will set the stage for your complete experience. Finding a venue that will match your style and deliver the level of service you require is similar to finding the right environment for filming a special scene in a movie. I'm sure you've seen movies where the characters are supposed to be driving through the outskirts of Seattle or in the English countryside, but instead it's obvious that they're driving through the hillsides of Southern California. Choosing the wrong venue can cause similar problems in the overall continuity of your wedding reception plans. Don't compromise or settle for less. Choose the location that not only fits your style, but will also help facilitate a better experience for you and your guests.

. . . .

POINTS TO CONSIDER

Choosing the reception location that will fit your needs and fulfill your vision can be a daunting task. Some places may be too big while others are too small. Some locations may look beautiful but have horrible acoustics. Some sites can offer you the world while others may feel like they are maintained by beings from another planet. Here are some helpful questions that may guide you in selecting the location that is just right for your wedding reception.

How far is your reception location from your ceremony site?
Too great a distance between the two locations can be a big problem. Guests might attend the ceremony but skip out on your reception, or they might get lost or stuck in traffic on the way to the reception.

What are the location's time restrictions?
Some locations do multiple events per day and require you to fit into their schedule. You may have to choose between a noon to 4:00 p.m. time slot or a 6:00 to 10:00 p.m. slot. Other locations may do only one event a day, giving you far

more flexibility. Some locations may have a four-hour maximum while others offer unlimited time. Some may prefer a four- to five-hour block of time to start, with an option to extend your celebration for an additional fee.

How early can your vendors arrive?

Most locations will allow 90 minutes as a minimum with up to two or three hours of lead time for your vendors to set up and decorate. Some locations may allow only one hour, but if there is an earlier function in the room, your vendors will be lucky if they are given even 30 minutes to get completely set up. This can make your vendors appear to be running late, when actually the situation has been entirely beyond their control.

How late can your reception last before you have to close down?

Some locations have noise restrictions after 10:00 p.m. due to local ordinances. If you want the option to have your reception last until midnight or later, this bit of information will play a crucial role in finding the right location. And if you want a specific length of time for your reception, learning about the noise restrictions will help you decide when to begin.

Additionally, some locations may be in the habit of "tearing down" the room when it best suits their needs. While the guests are still dancing, the staff may begin

Chinese Lanterns under the Stars

Evan and Christine celebrated their reception on his parents' ranch in Solvang. Just a year earlier, when we met to discuss their plans for the first time, we took a walk down into the dry gully next to Evan's parents' home to survey their proposed location. It took some imagination then, but with a little grading, a fresh layer of green grass, and some Chinese lanterns draped overhead, the dry gully was transformed into a fantastic setting for a memorable party.

* "NFL THEME"

Evan and Christine first met while going to school at Cal Poly San Luis Obispo (CPSLO). To make their garter toss more fun, they both autographed a CPSLO Mustangs football. Then Evan wrapped the garter around the football before tossing it into the air so the single guys could scramble for it.

RECEPTION AGENDA

6:00–7:20
Drinks & Appetizers

7:20
Grand Entrance
"Celebration"
by Kool & The Gang

7:30–8:40
Toasts & Dinner

8:40–9:00
The Special Dances
First Dance
"Sea Breeze"
by Tyrone Wells

Father/Daughter Dance
"Because You Loved Me"
by Celine Dion

Mother/Son Dance
"I Hope You Dance"
by Lee Ann Womack

Parents &
Wedding Party Dance
"The Way You Look Tonight"
by Frank Sinatra

9:00–9:30
Open Dancing

9:30
Cake Cutting
"Grow Old With You"
by Adam Sandler
"Ice Cream"
by Sarah McLachlan

9:40
Bouquet & Garter Toss
"Girls Just Want To Have Fun"
by Cyndi Lauper
"You Sexy Thing"
by Hot Chocolate
"Bad Boys (Cops Theme)"
by Inner Circle
"Mission: Impossible Theme"
by Larry Mullen & Adam Clayton
* *"NFL Theme" by Scott Schreer*

9:50–11:15
Open Dancing

11:15
Last Dance
"Good Riddance" by Green Day

clearing centerpieces, pulling table linens, and stacking chairs. This can give your guests the impression that your celebration is ending earlier than you had intended. Some locations have even been known to flip on their room lights during the last song because their contracted ending time has arrived. They might just as well have announced, "That's it! Time's up! Everybody out!" Be sure to clarify with your location when they will begin their tearing down process. And check to see if they will wait to turn up their lights until the reception has officially concluded.

How close is the reception location to the majority of your guests' homes?

If most of your guests are traveling over 30 minutes just to attend your reception, they may be inclined to leave earlier than you'd like because they have a long drive ahead of them. However, if your reception is located close to where the majority of your guests live, they will be more inclined to stay longer. If many of your guests are staying in a hotel, as in a destination wedding, your reception's proximity to that hotel should be carefully considered as well.

How many people can fit comfortably?

Some locations may be able to fit only a limited number of your guests in the main room, while requiring the rest of the guests be placed in an overflow room or patio. This can cause some of your guests to feel disconnected from the celebration. On the other side of the coin, if the room is too large, your guests may feel too spread out and it may be more difficult to get them involved when it's time to dance. Similar concerns should be raised when considering a tent (what size do you need?) or an outdoor setting.

Is there enough parking for all of your guests?

If not, you may want to consider hiring a valet service so your guests aren't delayed because they are hunting for parking spaces.

Is electrical power available for the musicians and/or DJ?

Some reception sites, like public parks, feature no power supply at all. A quiet generator may be required for amplified PA support and music. Some sites have power, but at a considerable distance from where the musicians and/or DJ may be setting up. Knowing how long an extension cord for power will be required can prevent any mishaps on the big day.

Is there any history of radio interference with wireless microphones in the area?

Some reception locations may have a well-documented history of radio interference that can interfere with the use of cordless microphones. If the location is close to the ocean or a military base, you may want to inform your

Choosing a Ceremony Site

If you and/or your fiancé had a religious upbringing, then getting married in a church or a synagogue might be your first choice. Many wedding ceremonies also occur in alternative locations, such as country clubs, banquet facilities, public parks, and private homes. Here are some important points to keep in mind as you select a site.

• How far is it from the reception site?

• Are there any restrictions on the timing of your ceremony?

• Is there enough parking for all your guests?

• If you need electricity for a sound system, is it available? Will you need to get a generator?

• Will your guests be able to sit down during the ceremony? If not, will that be a problem for some people?

• Is there any history of radio interference with wireless microphones in the area?

• Is there nearby traffic that could add unwanted noise during your ceremony?

• Is the location available for your wedding rehearsal when you want? If at all possible, make sure your rehearsal space and time is guaranteed in your contract.

• Does the location provide a ceremony coordinator, or are you required to provide a qualified coordinator as a prerequisite for using the location?

• Will the location's coordinator work as a team player with your other vendors? Interview other vendors who have worked with the coordinator to find out.

• Will the location's coordinator allow you to create your own ceremony schedule?

• Will the location's coordinator direct your ceremony rehearsal? If so, make sure that this person is willing to do some advance planning with you well before the rehearsal.

entertainment provider, especially if a cordless microphone will be used for the formal toasts.

If the reception location is outdoors, what are the precautions for bad weather?
Some locations may have a tent and space heaters as a backup for inclement weather while others may need to move the celebration indoors. If a backup plan is not

already in place, bad weather could put a damper on your day and your budget. Some tents come equipped with side walls that can be rolled up when the temperature is warm and rolled down in the event of cold weather, wind, or rain. If your location is outdoors and the weather is bright and sunny with sweltering heat, a lack of table umbrellas may leave your guests soaking in sweat well before the dancing even begins.

If the reception is indoors, are the environmental controls reliable?

A room without heat on a cold winter night or a room with no air conditioning on a hot summer afternoon can both make for an unbearable reception. Ask if the location has appropriate and reliable environmental control systems in place. You may even want to verify what the preferred temperature settings will be throughout the celebration.

What are the options for controlling the natural and electric lighting?

If your reception is during the day, and your location has large bay windows that cannot be covered with drapes or shades, your guests will be dancing in the daylight. A brightly lit room and exuberant dancing are usually not a good combination, although a qualified entertainer can still render a good response. But if shades can be drawn to block out some of the daylight, the effect will create the illusion of an evening reception, which will create a better atmosphere for dancing. If the location has only fluorescent lighting and no dimmer switches, creating the right atmosphere for your reception may be a bit of a challenge. Test out the lighting and see what settings are available. Ideally, the room lights can be set to an appropriate level for dinner and maybe even a darker setting for dancing at the end of the evening.

Can your entertainment be set up next to the dance floor?

Believe it or not, some locations actually require your entertainment to set up in a back corner or on a remote stage with tables of guests who are then unfortunately located between the speakers and the dance floor. This not only prevents the dance floor from attaining the appropriate volume levels for enthusiastic dancing, but it also forces the guests at these unlucky tables to suffer extremely high volume levels throughout the reception.

Does the room layout allow for a centrally located dance floor?

Upon viewing a country club for an upcoming reception, I was informed by the club's catering manager that the dance floor was usually set up at one end or the other of this basic rectangular room. When I asked if they had ever set up the dance floor in the center of the room, the manager said, "Oh no, that would just leave a big hole in the middle of the room." What she saw as a "big hole" is in reality "center stage" for most traditional wedding reception events. If your dance floor is at one end of a long room, in a separate room, or around a corner, your guests may feel left out when it is time for your first dance or the bouquet toss. A centrally located dance floor is easy to access for dancing, is more accessible for guests who want to watch the traditional events, is convenient for the catering staff as a place for staging the trays of food they will be serving, and will go a long way towards making everyone feel more involved. If the location you are considering does not already offer a centrally located dance floor, ask if it is willing to try such a layout for your reception. The following layout diagrams might be helpful:

OPTIMAL ROOM LAYOUTS

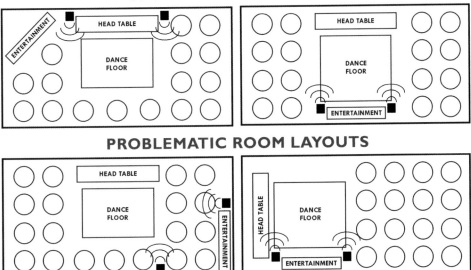

PROBLEMATIC ROOM LAYOUTS

If you choose a buffet service, will the number of buffet lines be increased to accommodate a larger guest count?

If you have one buffet line for over 200 guests, be prepared for the buffet service to last well over an hour. As your guest count grows, locations that are prepared to handle the increased number of guests will typically add buffet lines to allow more guests to be served in a shorter period of time. A buffet dinner that drags on unnecessarily long can put a damper on the overall mood of your reception.

Does the location require you to use its on-staff coordinator?

Keep in mind that some on-staff location coordinators may have their location's preferences and agenda prioritized higher than your own.

Will the location's coordinator allow you to create your own reception schedule?

It is vital that you find this out in advance. If the location's preferences have been set up to facilitate its needs, the reception may lack the flow you prefer. One location had a policy of requiring the bride and groom to cut their cake right after the grand entrance and the toasts so it could be served as dessert and some of the catering staff could be sent home, thus saving on payroll costs. Although this idea is not necessarily wrong, it may not suit your own preferences and style. Don't let your location dictate your reception timeline if it clashes with your own ideas. After all, this is your wedding reception, not theirs.

What is the location's policy regarding their preferred vendors list?

Most locations have a list of preferred vendors whom they are happy to recommend based on professionalism and quality of service that they have witnessed. These locations recognize that professional vendors who provide a quality service in a reliable manner not only do right by their clients, but they also make the location look good in return. Other locations, however, will refer vendors who offer them a finder's fee or are willing to put the location's agenda preferences above those of their clients. In some rare occasions, the location may actually attach an additional "damage deposit" or penalty fee for using vendors who are not on their preferred vendor list. Read the fine print before signing a contract to secure such a location. These added fees are designed to encourage you to choose their preferred vendors, who may not be either the best qualified or the right vendors for your needs. Don't let anyone force you to choose vendors you are not completely comfortable hiring.

How many events will be occurring at the location during your reception?

In some rare occasions, certain locations may host four or more ceremonies and/or receptions on the same premises at the same time. Not only can this lead to possible confusion for your guests and/or vendors, but it can put a damper on your celebration as well.

I had the unique opportunity to participate in a wedding ceremony and reception at a location that can best be described as a wedding factory. My clients were holding their ceremony at the location's gazebo, which was a mere 80 feet from the open courtyard where their reception was to be held. This courtyard was surrounded by a four-foot-high hedge. We were notified by the location just three days before the wedding that they had two more ceremonies scheduled for the gazebo during my client's reception. We were told we would have to turn down our music during both ceremonies. Needless to say, this was not only disconcerting and distressing for my clients, but it was also rather daunting news for me. After weighing our options, I advised my clients that we could schedule certain parts of their reception agenda to allow for the music to be turned down without causing much negative impact on their reception. Because we knew when the two wedding ceremonies were scheduled to begin, we adjusted the beginning of the meal to coincide perfectly with the start of the first ceremony. Having the background music play lower than normal during dinner was a great solution.

I suggested we start my clients' money dance just before the next ceremony so the lower music volume would once again fit the moment. Our timing was perfect and we started the money dance right on schedule. Unfortunately, the second ceremony didn't get started for another 15 minutes. So our money dance ended before the second ceremony was over and the low volume we were required to maintain was not conducive for a dancing atmosphere. As a result, their reception ended earlier than we all would have liked, and my clients were very upset with the location's management.

Set Design Details to Consider

Many books and magazines advise you about style, design, and décor for weddings and receptions, but they rarely give you advice from the perspective of your entertainment. Here are four common "set design" details that can impact your entertainment.

Overgrown centerpieces

Avoid choosing centerpieces that are too large and block your guests' line of sight. If your guests can't clearly see the person seated across the table from them, not only will table conversations be impeded, but many of them will not be able to see the grand entrance, the formal toasts, or your first dance. Choose smaller centerpieces or put the larger centerpiece on a tall, narrow stand to open the sight lines throughout the room.

Room to jump around

Don't use low-hanging decorations over the dance floor. Decorative tulle twisted with twinkle lights can create a nice look, but if it is hanging too low over the dance floor, it can be easily damaged when the dancing gets underway.

Burning up

Flammable decorations and votive candles can be both beautiful and dangerous at the same time. If you use votive candles for decorative purposes, be sure to put them in containers that are taller than the candle's flame. Some candles tend to be smoky, so give them a test burn before you commit to using them. And of course, check with your location on restrictions regarding candles and open flames.

Shedding a little light

If the location offers colored up-lighting to change the ambience of the room, the lights should be on dimmer switches so the brightness can be adjusted throughout the reception. Consider all the special moments that will happen throughout your reception and make sure the lighting can be adjusted appropriately throughout the event. If a room's lighting has to be significantly dimmed to enhance the effect of spotlights, other events taking place throughout the room may be left in the dark. If spot lighting or other special lighting effects are too bright, the energy on the dance floor could be negatively affected. Wedding Entertainment Director Mike Anderson adds, "With the latest in LED lighting technology, you can now choose colored up-lighting that is battery powered. These lights run cooler and can be controlled wirelessly to change the color schemes as desired."

< no >

CHAPTER 5
SCREENING THE CINEMATOGRAPHERS
Evaluating Your Photographer and Videographer

*W*hen a movie director yells, "Cut! That's a wrap!" it usually means that the principal filming has been finished for the day. But we are also familiar with the terms, "Take 2…Take 3," when an actor is asked to redo a scene until the director feels the right moment has been captured. On your wedding day, however, some special moments need to be captured with no opportunity for a "Take 2." Finding the right photographer to capture those moments in a style that matches your desires can be downright challenging. Choosing a videographer can be equally difficult. To help you make those choices, this chapter focuses specifically on how your photographer and videographer can impact the entertainment at your reception.

THE SCREENING PROCESS

As with any talent-based profession, there are professional photographers and videographers and there are some who are less than professional. The pros will dress appropriately, return your calls, and treat your needs with the respect and timeliness you deserve. They will be experienced in working with other vendors as a team player and capturing the special moments that you will look back on for years to come. If capturing your memories with photos and on video is important to you, don't cut corners. Choose a true professional you can count on to document your day without hampering the success of your reception experience.

Here are some helpful points to consider that may guide you in selecting the photographer and/or videographer who fits your style and needs.

Shutter drag
Most wedding photographers can finish your post-ceremony family, wedding party, and romantic shots in 45 minutes to an hour. But if the photographer you

select takes two hours, and your guests are left waiting along with the chef, the party atmosphere at your reception can take a dive very quickly. As you interview photographers, ask each one about his time requirements, and be sure to ask his references how timely he actually was on the wedding day. At a recent reception, the photographer told me he would be taking the bride and groom out for some "quick" sunset photos. Ninety minutes later, when they finally returned, only 20 percent of their guests were still waiting. If the guests of honor are gone too long from a reception, many guests will perceive this as a green light to make their exit.

Photojournalists vs. posers

Photographers who specialize in the popular photojournalistic approach tend to stay out of the way as they capture candid moments and emotions. Other photographers, who prefer to pose their shots, can vary in their level of involvement. For example, some will motion from a distance for the bride and groom to both look at the camera during their first dance, while others may make them stop dancing and adjust their positions and the direction their faces are turned before taking the shot. The latter example can have a dramatic impact on the flow of your reception, especially if this type of "poser" has to set up each and every shot this way. Of course, you should secure the photographer whose style and results match your expectations, but if his photos are mostly posed and look stiff or contrived, ask how involved he gets in setting up his shots.

Video reenactments

Similarly, some videographers can cause delays of their own by insisting on shooting two or three additional "takes" of a memorable moment. Perhaps they failed to get the footage they needed the first time, or maybe they are trying to get different angles to simulate a two-camera shoot. Regardless of the reason, it will not only cost you time and slow down the pace of your reception, but it can also turn a spontaneous moment into one that feels contrived and uncomfortable. If your cake cutting, for example, turns into 15 minutes of filming "video reenactments," your guests may begin to lose interest. Before you hire a videographer, ask if he makes a habit of shooting "video reenactments."

Tick tock, tick tock

How long is your photographer contracted to stay at your reception? If your photographer's contracted service time ends much earlier than your reception, you may not have anyone available to capture some of your special moments on film. If the photographer begins pressuring your entertainment to "speed things up" so he can finish on time per his contract, this can lead to an agenda that feels rushed. If you prefer not to pay to have your photographer stay until the reception ends, at least schedule for him to stay until all of your festivities have been completed without having to rush. But if you can afford to hire a photographer who will stay until your reception ends, I would highly recommend it. I can't tell you how many fun and unexpected moments I have seen occur during the last hour of dancing at a reception that were never captured by the photographer (or videographer). This can be especially disappointing if you have a festive sendoff planned and no one is there to professionally capture those moments on film.

Blinded by the light

Find out in advance what lighting the videographer uses. Most professionals use camera lights that can be adjusted from dim to bright. But if the videographer has a camera light that features only one setting—extra bright—not only will many of your images get washed out, but people may also be scared away from the dance floor. I have seen the father of the bride coming out for the father/daughter dance with his hand shielding his eyes because the videographer's light was too bright. I've also seen videographers filming the guests dancing from less than a foot away (attempting to get American Bandstand–style footage) with a light so bright that the guests left the dance floor. The real pros use the best tools and they know how to use them to capture the footage they need without intruding on, or disrupting, your celebration.

Flexible team players

Before hiring a photographer and/or videographer, be sure to ask if they will be willing to discuss the photography schedule with your entertainment vendor in

advance of the reception. If your photographer and/or videographer are not flexible team players, miscommunication may result. If your photographer plans to do a large group photo but doesn't communicate in advance with your entertainment about this, a smooth-flowing agenda may be suddenly disrupted. By communicating with your entertainment about these details before your big day, not only will the photographer and/or videographer get the shots they want, but also their requests will be incorporated into your agenda.

You should also check with your entertainment to make sure they will keep your videographer informed before starting any activities that may need to be captured on video.

CHAPTER 6

AUDITIONING FOR TALENT

Filling Your Primary Supporting Roles: Band, DJ, or Master of Ceremonies

. . . .

*W*hen a new movie is getting ready to begin production in Hollywood, there's usually a buzz about its lead actors and primary supporting actors. The two of you, as the bride and groom, are already filling the lead roles, but a strong team of supporting actors can help you carry off an Oscar-worthy, unforgettable celebration. This chapter explores various options for your primary supporting actors — your entertainment vendors — and the points you need to seriously consider when selecting them. You'll learn how to find the best wedding entertainment by asking the right questions and by taking the time to meet with the vendors in person. You'll learn to choose the people with the talents you find appealing, the skills to turn your dreams into reality, and the personality to entertain your guests in a style and manner that will fulfill and exceed your expectations. Not only will your guests enjoy themselves more, but they will also be raving for months to come that yours was "The Best Wedding Reception…Ever!"

. . . .

LIVE BANDS

Live bands have been providing music and entertainment at wedding celebrations since the invention of musical instruments. Some bands are great, many are best described as typical, and others can be just plain awful. If you are considering hiring a live band for your wedding entertainment, here are some important benefits:

- Live bands can usually play music really well.

- Live bands can bring a lot of energy into a room.

- Live bands can do medleys and extended jam sessions of songs.

Live bands are second to none when it comes to creating energy that can get your crowd up and moving on the dance floor. When they see that a song is getting an enthusiastic reaction from your guests, they can often keep that song going longer than normal. Many bands are skilled at creating medleys that blend from one song and/or genre into another on the fly. They can also help you create a specific environment. If you want to create a swing/big band theme, a ten-piece orchestra with a crooner style singer might be just the ticket.

However, there are important questions to be answered during your band interviewing and selecting process.

How will the band perform your special songs?

Every band will play, in their own way, the songs you have selected. Even the best cover bands are just imitating the original artists. Some bands will take a song from the '50s rock-and-roll era and perform it as a reggae song instead. When you select the song for your first dance, what will prompt your decision? Does it remind you of the time when the two of you first met? Do the lyrics clearly communicate your current feelings for each other? Whatever contributes to your decisions for all of the special songs you want to hear on your wedding day, be aware that a live band will not play the songs exactly as you remember them. The instrumentation may be similar, the vocals may even be close to the original artist's recording, but a band will still perform your songs their way. Ask to see a demo or an audition of the band performing your first dance selection. This opportunity might also give you a better understanding of their unique style.

How many songs and genres can the band currently perform?

Does the band have the talent and skill to perform the diverse range of musical genres needed to make your party happen? Some bands are limited to only one or two specific genres. If they are not up to date with the current hit songs for dancing, they might not appeal to your younger guests. If they are strong on the new music but limited on the classics and the oldies, your older guests might feel left out. Of course, if you are creating a theme, then specific genre limitations might be a perfect fit for your needs.

Who will be making the announcements at your reception?

Just because someone can sing doesn't necessarily mean he or she is qualified to serve as your spokesperson. Specialized talent and skill are required to be an exceptional master of ceremonies at a wedding reception. Just think of all the talent and stars the Academy considers when choosing a host for the Oscars. Even after several months of preparation, the chosen host doesn't always get the best reviews. The best MCs make the job look effortless, but there is always an incredible amount of preparation behind the scenes.

Being a great musician takes years of training and practice combined with unique talent and specialized skills. However, all of this work and talent may not matter much when it's time to announce your wedding party's grand entrance. When considering a live band, it is imperative that you find out what training the band's MC has to be an effective spokesperson. Ask to hear sample announcements as an audition. Everyone auditions the music, but how many people overlook the capabilities of the MC? If the announcements are generic in nature, such as referring to you as the bride and groom or the happy couple, instead of using your first names, then your guests will experience a very impersonal presentation from the MC. Don't wait until your wedding day to find out that your singer isn't qualified to serve as your spokesperson.

Can you see uncut video footage of announcements they have made at other weddings?

Be sure to ask for video footage of the band in action. It will undoubtedly show guests dancing and enjoying themselves as the band plays great tunes. But watch carefully and look for the special moments in the reception that require clear, concise, and polished announcements. If the band is only showing you edited footage, without any announcements, insist on seeing footage, or an audition, of how they will announce your special moments.

What is their policy on taking breaks during a reception?

Playing live music is hard work. It can be downright exhausting. But most bands have a solution for this predictable dilemma. It is called break time. Imagine your dance floor is fully packed with friends and family members who are dancing to their heart's content when the band leader suddenly announces, "Ummm, folks, we're gonna take a break...we'll be back in about 15 minutes." Now what?

What happens next will vary depending on the band. They may take a break, with no music playing for the next 15 minutes, and many of your guests may decide that it is time to leave. They may throw on a background CD and just let it play unattended during their break. Many of your guests may leave. They may have a DJ on site to play requests during their breaks. But truly talented DJs will rarely give up their prime dates to play band breaks. So the question needs to be asked: Can the band's DJ measure up to the task? Ask for references and video footage of their DJ in action.

A better solution is for the band to bring along extra musicians so their members can take individual breaks throughout your reception while the rest of the band plays on. This solution keeps the energy going. As you might expect, a wedding band with enough members to pull this off will likely cost more than a band with fewer members.

What is their policy on meals?

Some bands may insist on being fed during your reception. Some may even request being fed the same meal as your guests, which can lead to an unexpected increase on your catering bill. If your band requires food, but not necessarily the same meal as your guests, be sure to ask your catering contact if they will provide a less expensive "vendor meal" for the band members.

How will they prevent dead air from occurring at your reception?

One of the worst mistakes you can make on radio is dead air. Dead air is when the cue for the next commercial, song, or announcement is missed, and the listeners hear nothing at all for several seconds or even minutes. Dead air is also a serious issue when considering a live band. If you ask to view a demo video, you can rest assured that there will be no dead air left for you to see. Be proactive, however, and ask to see an uncut video of the band in action so you can watch how well they transition from one song to the next.

A great wedding band should be ready to play after toasts and other special events, and they should keep the music going seamlessly without taking breaks or pausing to determine which song they should play next. Imagine a great song ending and as the crowd is applauding, the band members begin to discuss among themselves what song they should play next. While they are busy talking, the dead air becomes uncomfortable and the guests, who are now just standing on the dance floor, begin to walk back to

their tables. Just as they reach their seats, the band strikes up with another song and some of the guests come back and begin to dance again. Repeat that process several times. Soon your guests will begin to grow tired of the dead air between songs and many of them will begin to head for the door.

What responsibility will the band take for directing the pacing and flow of your reception's agenda?

When it comes to managing the pacing and flow of your reception's agenda, who's directing? (This subject is covered in greater detail in Chapter 7: "Nominating the Best Director.") A live band will be able to play music and might even make the announcements for you, but will they be able to play their instruments and guide and direct your reception events at the same time? Who will make sure that the cake knife is at the cake table before your cake cutting is announced? Who will let your parents know in advance to be ready for their special dances with you? A typical wedding band won't have the time, manpower, or skill to direct your reception because their job is primarily to play the music.

If a band says they will direct your reception's events, ask them to tell you how. If this is a service they regularly offer, they should be able to show you their detailed reception direction checklist. If not, they are most likely winging it and hoping nothing will go wrong. Experience has shown that those who "wing it" tend to run into problems more often than those who are prepared and double-check the details.

How will they communicate with the other vendors about your agenda while they are performing?

Ideally, the band will have an assistant who can discuss agenda details with the other vendors and then cue the band when needed. If your band does not have someone filling this role, they most likely will rely on your coordinator or catering director to keep them informed. Someone has to do this, however, or you may run into more dead air as the band is left to figure out for themselves what they should be doing or playing next.

Can the band's volume levels be turned down if requested?

Some bands start off loud, stay loud, and then just get louder. Be sure to ask the band if they are willing to turn down their volume if and when it is requested. If your guests have to shout to carry on a conversation during dinner, the music is too loud and many of your guests will be turned off.

What can they tell you about their service and performance that sets them apart from all the rest?

A live band that regularly entertains at weddings should be ready to answer this question confidently and specifically. Perhaps they offer the option of personalizing your first dance selection with updated lyrics that feature your first names. Maybe they have some fun suggestions for creating memorable involvement among your guests during the dancing. Or they might be able to wear outfits that complement the color scheme and theme for your reception. Give them a chance to share their unique services and capabilities and you just might find yourself even more thrilled with choosing them to provide your entertainment.

The Ceremony Minstrels

If you are thinking about hiring live musicians to play the music for your wedding ceremony, consider:

Can the singers really sing?

There's nothing worse than a singer who is off-key and doesn't know the words during a wedding ceremony. Ask to hear a demo tape, view a demo video, or see an audition before making any final decisions. Also, make sure they have their own instrumental music CD if there will be no live musicians.

Will the musicians have your ceremony sheet music in a separate binder?

Some musicians bring one oversized binder holding the sheet music for every song they can play. But if the actual ceremony songs are not in a separate binder, there may be lengthy delays between songs as the musicians flip through their entire sheet music library to find the next piece. This delay can be easily avoided if the musicians have taken the time to prepare a separate folder in advance, featuring just your ceremony music selections.

Can the musicians wrap up a song early if needed?

An unexpected delay in a wedding ceremony can occur when the live musicians are unable to wrap up a song early and have to finish the entire piece of music while the bride is standing in front of the officiant and everyone is ready for the ceremony to commence. Be sure to ask if the musicians you are considering have the confidence, skill, and experience to wrap up your ceremony selections at the appropriate time.

Do your ceremony musicians have the amplification to match your guest count?

Depending on your guest count, your musicians may need additional sound support and amplification. If you have more than 300 guests, a string quartet may not be able to create enough volume all on their own. If you have singers and/or other musicians, they may need additional microphones and an extra person managing the audio mixer. If they don't have the equipment and/or personnel to meet these needs, you will need to seek out professional audio support.

THE WEDDING DISC JOCKEY

Mobile disc jockeys (DJs who travel with portable sounds systems) have been providing music and entertainment at wedding celebrations since the early 1970s, when they first emerged as a less expensive alternative to live bands. When disc jockeys first began entertaining at receptions, their primary focus was on playing prerecorded music for the dancing. Some companies expanded their services by offering disco lighting. Others hired additional DJs so they could cover multiple clients and events simultaneously. And some expanded their services to include the master of ceremonies duties. (In Canada, some disc jockeys are just now starting to offer master of ceremonies services because culturally, the best man or a family friend has usually been asked to fill that role.) In the 1990s, some disc jockeys became "party motivators" who were skilled at teaching and leading creative and interactive group dances. Others expanded their services by offering more assistance with the planning and overall direction of the reception's pacing and flow. And finally, some DJs started offering uniquely personalized entertainment designed to keep the focus on the bride and groom.

With all of this variety available, it is disconcerting to note that the overall perception about DJs in regards to wedding celebrations is typically negative. Words like "cheesy" or "obnoxious" are often used to describe bad DJ entertainment. Part of this overall negative perception might be related to the fact that a large majority of mobile disc jockeys in the United States are currently DJing as a sideline business while working in an unrelated full-time career. With limited time to invest in their performance, many of them are stuck in a cycle of mediocrity. But there are talented DJs available if you know how and where to find them.

If you are considering hiring a DJ to provide the entertainment at your wedding reception, here are some important benefits to consider:

- Disc jockeys can mix prerecorded music really well.

- Disc jockeys can play a wide variety of music genres.

- Disc jockeys can keep your celebration flowing smoothly.

Disc jockeys have the advantage of being able to play just about any genre of music you've requested, while being able to change gears on a moment's notice to adjust to your guests' reactions. A really talented DJ will not only read your crowd, but he will also lead and direct your guests with both his music selections and his announcements. A talented DJ can help you create a fun reception that will keep your guests entertained for the duration of your celebration.

SEPTEMBER 12, 2009
MONARCH BEACH, CALIFORNIA

The Best of Both Worlds

Drew and Jessi both love live music, but they also wanted to roast their wedding party members during their grand entrance. With the St. Regis Monarch Beach Resort as their ceremony and reception location, they were also in need of a polished master of ceremonies. Band or a DJ? They said, "We'll take both!" In addition to my entertainment services, they brought in "The Spazmatics," a fun, energetic '80s cover band whose members dress up like nerds and geeks. When the formal festivities were concluded, the band took over and put on an amazingly entertaining show.

* TOASTS

Drew and Jessi's best man, Terry, surprised everyone in the middle of his toast when he cued me to start playing an instrumental track from a rap song. And then he began to "bust a rhyme" he had written in tribute to his best friend. The guests cheered and Drew and Jessi looked pleasantly surprised by his uniquely creative toast.

RECEPTION AGENDA

7:15
Grand Entrance
"1980" by Rehab

7:25
First Dance
"Huckleberry" by Toby Keith

7:30
*Toasts

7:50–8:50
Dinner

8:50
Video Montage

9:00–9:15
The Special Dances
Father/Daughter Dance
"Cinderella"
by Steven Curtis Chapman
Mother/Son Dance
"(Everything I Do) I Do It For You"
by Bryan Adams
Wedding Party Dance
"Let's Get Married"
by Jagged Edge & Run

9:15–10:00
Open Dancing

10:00
CupCake Cutting
"The Way You Make Me Feel"
by Michael Jackson

10:15
Bouquet & Garter Toss
"Girls On The Dance Floor"
by Far East Movement

"Good Girls Go Bad"
by Cobra Starship

"Bad To The Bone"
by George Thorogood
& The Destroyers

"Love Machine (Part I)"
by The Miracles

"I'm Shipping Up To Boston"
by Dropkick Murphys

10:25–12:00 (a.m.)
Open Dancing

12:00 (a.m.)
Last Dance
"I Party"
by Far East Movement
feat. Iz & DB Tonic

However, there are some important questions you should ask as you interview and select a DJ.

If you go through a DJ company, will you be guaranteed to get the DJ that you want? Will his name be listed on the contract?

If the DJ company is unwilling to list the specific DJ you have selected by name on the contract, then perhaps they are not willing to guarantee who will actually be the DJ at your reception. This should be cause for alarm. If you develop a good rapport with a DJ, but on the day of your reception, you are greeted by one of that DJ's subordinates with no advance warning, you may be in for a bumpy ride. Unfortunately, some DJs treat wedding receptions like "gigs." They will book as many "gigs" as they can get, and then send out an employee or a subcontractor with a story about why the other DJ was not available. The tactic is called "bait and switch" and it has been a blight on the DJ industry for far too long. You should expect and demand that the entertainer you choose be named and guaranteed in the contract. Your reception entertainment is too important to be left in the hands of a total stranger.

Is the DJ a member of any industry trade associations?

Joining a trade association shows you that the DJ is committed to not only improving his own services, but it also demonstrates that he is committed to helping improve the industry as a whole. Joining a trade association typically doesn't require any "proof" of a DJ's level of talent or professional status, but the desire to become more skilled or attain professional status is usually encouraged by such associations. What this means to brides and grooms is that being a trade association member is not verification of a DJ's capabilities or quality of service, but it does show his commitment to ongoing education and training. As a former national president of the American Disc Jockey Association (ADJA), I highly recommend searching for prospective DJs who are currently on the association's membership roster. The ADJA offers local chapters with monthly meetings and provides educational content designed to help DJs of all skill levels improve their services and performances. You can look for a local ADJA member in your area by visiting their Web site (http://ADJA.org). There are many other local and national DJ associations available, and a simple Internet search should help you locate any groups in your region.

How many songs can you select for your ceremony and/or reception?

The correct answer should be "all of them," but you may get a variety of different answers to this question. Because this is your celebration, your input and opinions on the music selections should be given top priority. But some DJs will ask you to pick ten songs for dancing and then insist that you just trust them to format the rest of the selections. If you trust this DJ, or have little opinion about your dancing music selections, you may have found a good match for your needs. However, if you are particular about your music choices, you may want to seek a DJ that is willing to give you complete input.

There are three primary categories of music to consider when planning your musical selections. The first category — background music selections — is the music that will be playing as your guests are arriving for your ceremony, at your cocktail hour, and during the meal. This area of musical selection, more than just about any other, tends to get swept under the rug by many DJs who prefer to play the same background mix at all of their receptions. Don't be afraid to insist on seeing a list of types of background music from your DJ. If he is unable to produce

Crashing Weddings

Many bridal magazines and books over the years have encouraged brides to request an opportunity to see their prospective band or DJ in action at an actual wedding reception. This advice is not only misguided, it can be downright harmful to the current couple/clients as well as the prospective couple/clients. When a band or a DJ is performing at a wedding reception, they are "on stage" for at least four hours, if not much longer. When a prospective couple/client drops by to watch them in action, they will typically witness only twenty minutes of the total performance. Depending on where the band or DJ is in the overall agenda, the visiting couple might only see them playing background music during the meal. If the band or DJ is aware that the prospective couple/client is there, their focus may become split between fulfilling their current couple/client's agenda and auditioning for their prospective couple/client. Strangers should never be allowed to crash your own wedding reception, so don't crash someone else's reception. There are much better ways to verify the skills and talents of a band or a DJ.

such a list, then perhaps his background selections are severely limited or maybe he just prefers to make such decisions without your input.

The second category — your special moments music selections — is the music that plays as you are walking down the aisle during your wedding ceremony as well as the special dances and events during the reception. These are often the most memorable music-related moments of a wedding and these songs should be determined by you and you alone. If you want the traditional "Bridal March" by Richard Wagner, then your DJ's next question should be, "Which version would you prefer?" Whether it's your first dance selection, your choice for the father/daughter dance, or the songs that play as you cut your cake or toss your bouquet, these are your moments and you should be able to choose the soundtrack that fits your personal style. Be sure to ask your DJ for a list of ceremony music suggestions as well as a list of suggested songs for your reception events. And feel free to come up with your own ideas for these moments as well. Music attaches itself to memories, and the songs you select for these moments will become a part of the memories you will carry with you for the rest of your life.

The third category — your dancing requests — is the music that plays during the open dancing at your reception. Again, your input and music preferences should be respected by your DJ. Once you have weighed in with your top requests, your favorite artists, and your "do not play" list, a professional DJ should be trusted to format your selections in order to create a mix of dancing music that will appeal to the varied tastes and age groups at your reception. Be sure to ask your DJ for a comprehensive list of popular suggested requests for dancing music to assist you in picking out music for dancing. If he balks at the notion, he might prefer to use his own selections without your input. This may mean that he has a proven track record of creating energetic dancing at receptions. But it could also be a warning flag that he prefers to play the same thirty to fifty songs that he always plays for dancing. (This explains why songs such as "YMCA" and "Old Time Rock & Roll" tend to get overplayed at weddings.) A talented DJ should be able to incorporate your top requests and your favorite artists (provided the artist's songs are danceable) while avoiding the songs on your "do not play" list. He should also be able to filter in requests from your guests while occasionally mixing in songs he knows will fit perfectly for your crowd in the moment. Be prepared to pick an average of fifteen to twenty songs for each hour of open dancing, but don't be afraid to select more than needed so your DJ will have plenty of requests to work with when the time comes.

What creative ideas can he share for making your reception more fun in a personalized way?

This question will help you identify whether the DJ believes that he just plays music, or if he recognizes the value of creating uniquely personalized entertainment. A DJ who still sees his job as "just music" will be more likely to treat your reception like a "gig" instead of seeking ways to create a personalized entertainment experience for you and your guests. A DJ should be able to not only list several unique and creative ideas, but he should also be able to help you develop ideas that will fit your reception perfectly. If a DJ is stumped by this question, he is probably only familiar with delivering an average, cookie-cutter style of reception entertainment.

What responsibility will he take for directing the pacing and flow of your reception's agenda?

Have you ever been a guest at a wedding reception that moved along far too slowly? When the pace of a reception is not properly directed, the guests get restless and may consider leaving early. Unfortunately, many DJs still show up to their events expecting someone else to direct the pacing and flow. Perhaps they are counting on the wedding coordinator for guidance or looking to the catering director for cues. But if they are not actively trying to maintain an entertaining flow, then your reception may be more likely to drag.

Because a smooth-flowing party will always result in more fun on the dance floor, many talented DJs have become proactive about helping to direct the timing and flow of their receptions. A top-notch DJ will prepare an entertainment agenda for your reception and then share copies of it with your location, your catering manager, coordinator, photographer, videographer, and the rest of your team. If everyone is informed of the entertainment schedule in advance, the DJ will be able to resolve any timing issues well before your big day. This part of a DJ's service begins to cross over into the services provided by a master of ceremonies.

Is the DJ familiar with your ceremony and/or reception location?

Because some locations have unique challenges, it is very important that your entertainment be familiar with the space and room layout provided by your location. If the DJ has worked at your location before, ask him if there were any unexpected problems with the room layout or with the location's preferred order of events. Ask him to explain how these obstacles were overcome or resolved.

At one ceremony and reception facility, the location would not allow the bride to take care of her own ceremony music and PA support through her entertainment vendor. Instead, they insisted on providing the PA support for the ceremony themselves and they only allowed the bride to hear her musical selections as played by their live pianist. When the bride pressed for more information, she was told that the owners of the facility felt that prerecorded music was "schlocky" and made their location look bad. Because the bride was set on hearing her own prerecorded selections, she cancelled with the location and moved to a facility that was more supportive of her desires. Knowing this, I will not sell my ceremony support services for this particular location, and I will gladly share this story with any bride who is considering having her ceremony at this particular location.

If the DJ has not worked at your location yet, be sure to ask if he will do a site visit before your big day. A DJ should insist on a site visit and may even request to schedule it with you present so any challenges can be discussed and resolved on the spot. Some locations may require extra speakers. Some locations may require some help to make the room layout more entertaining. If your DJ discovers these issues for the first time on your wedding day, he may be short on extra speakers or he may not have time to make any necessary adjustments to the room layout.

If your location has some unusual policies regarding the loading in of equipment, the volume levels during the reception, the setup area for the DJ, or even the set order of reception events, your DJ will need to know ahead of time. If the policies are too restrictive, you may find some of the better quality entertainers choosing to pass on working at such facilities.

One facility in my area will not allow the entertainment to begin loading in until one hour before the doors open for the guests. They require the entertainment to set up in a back corner, some 45 feet away from the dance floor, making it harder to create the right volume levels for dancing while, at the same time, blasting out the guests who are unfortunate enough to be seated between the speakers and the dance floor. This same facility will also require the bride and groom to cut their cake at the end of the meal, regardless of whether or not the bride and groom want to wait and cut their cake after some open dancing. This schedule is enforced so they can clear off the cake table for pitchers of water, iced tea, and lemonade. Because this location is so difficult to work with, I, and several other entertainers in my area, will not book receptions at it.

If you have not yet found your location, ask your DJ which locations he would recommend and then ask what makes them worth recommending. He might have some insights that you might not be able to get from any other source.

What can he tell you about his services and/or performance that sets him apart?

A talented DJ should be ready to answer this question with gusto. This question should also be asked of anyone who recommends a particular DJ to you. Keep in mind that most DJs do the same things, but it is how they do what they do that truly sets them apart. Most DJs return phone calls and e-mails. Some do it quickly and some will get back to you in few days. Most DJs will introduce your first dance. Some will do it in a very personalized way while others might say the same thing they have said at every reception for the last five years. If a DJ says he is the same as all of the rest, but he's just cheaper, this should tell you that he is relying on a low price as his primary attraction. The truth is, if he can do "the same things" in the same way that enables other DJs in his region to charge higher fees, increased demand for his services would enable him to charge just as much as other DJs.

What improvements has he made in his services and/or performance in the last two years?

Maintaining a competitive edge in a performance-based service industry requires constant, ongoing education and training. It's similar to running up the down escalator—if you stop running, you are losing ground. No performer, whether he is an actor, a musician, or a DJ, ever "arrives" or becomes completed as a performer. The very best DJs continue their education and training through performance workshops, seminars, trade shows, and involvement in their local and national trade associations. If a DJ is unable to give you a list of improvements he has made in his services and/or performance, chances are he has become complacent. It's very likely that he is delivering, at best, an average caliber of services and/or performance. A qualified DJ should be ready to answer this question with confidence because he is always improving. If the broader question stumps the DJ, try asking if he has

attended any national or local trade shows or performance workshops in the last two years.

Does he have feedback surveys that will verify his level of skill and talent?

Check references. Ask for feedback surveys. Take the time to read what previous clients had to say about the DJ's unique skills and talents. If he has feedback surveys but is not willing to share them with you, perhaps the feedback hasn't been as glowing as he'd like you to believe. Or maybe he is not currently seeking feedback from his clients. The best DJs will always look for feedback to help them continue to improve their services. Someone who isn't requesting feedback may be perfectly content with the level of service he is providing. In such a case, calling recent clients for their feedback would be highly recommended.

Can you see uncut video footage of the DJ performing at a reception?

Requesting uncut video footage is one of the best ways to verify the true skills and talents of a DJ. Uncut video footage will show you everything. If he is unwilling to share such footage, perhaps he has something to hide. Talented DJs not only seek feedback via surveys, but they will also often review uncut video footage of their own performances for the purpose of self-critique and personal improvement.

When you watch the footage, here are a few things to look for and keep in mind:

Watch his transitions. Is the DJ prepared for what comes next after each moment? Is he keeping the guests' attention focused? Does he appear unprepared? Is the DJ asking questions on the mic about whether it's time for the next agenda item? Does he have the right music ready for the next moment? Do the various events appear to be flowing smoothly, or are there long pauses between events that are filled with dead air? Keeping your party flowing smoothly requires a skilled entertainer who knows how to direct your events with seamless transitions. Choose the person you can trust to keep things on track.

Keep in mind that every reception celebration should be crafted uniquely for each couple. Some of the entertaining ideas you see on the video may be totally contrary to your personal style and tastes, but they may have been perfect for that particular couple. Don't let ideas that turn you off cause you to pass on a particular DJ. Look deeper and see if he has the talent and the skill to deliver the kind of entertainment that will be appropriate for you.

How will he create a full dance floor at your reception?

Every DJ should be able to describe his own "dance theory" for filling a dance floor with guests of all ages and tastes. If a DJ begins with statements like, "What I always do to get the dancing started is…," or "What I always play to get the dancing started is…," there is a high likelihood that he has a set play list or a set routine that he delivers the same way at all of his receptions. Some DJs will insist that their use of group dances has always been a surefire way to kick off the dancing. Some experienced DJs may suggest starting off with older selections that are still popular among all age groups while later in the night mixing in the newer music that tends to appeal to your younger guests. Still others might recommend starting off with a popular romantic slow song to bring up all the couples for a slow dance. Keep in mind that the only responses that are wrong are the ones that will not fit for you and/or your group. Some receptions need a group dance to get things kicked off. Others may turn into a dance party naturally during the course of the meal with no verbal encouragement from the DJ at all.

Are the DJ's prices below average, average, or above average, and why?

A DJ should always be able to clearly communicate the reasons for his pricing and the value that is provided. If his pricing is below average, he may be just getting into the business or DJing as a sideline. A lower than average price may also speak to the quality of the service a DJ is able to offer.

In reality, all wedding DJs do many of the same things, but how those things are done determines whether you are dealing with a talented DJ or just an average DJ. Pricing for wedding DJs is tied directly to their skill and talent levels, because the top performers will always see increased demand, thus allowing them to charge increasingly higher fees. An average DJ will not see as much demand and will remain stuck in the range of average pricing.

1

2

3

4

5

Will he and his equipment be presented in an appropriate manner?

One of the most common complaints about DJs at receptions is related to their apparel and the look of their equipment setups. Some amateur DJs have been known to show up at a reception in black jeans, sneakers, and a tuxedo-print T-shirt. But most talented DJs recognize that a formal celebration calls for formal attire. Granted, some couples may opt for a costumed theme or a casual dress code, but they will also undoubtedly request that their DJ dress to match the occasion. Ask to see photos of the DJ and/or his staff at a recent reception. Be clear with your DJ about your dress code expectations.

While you're at it, request to see some photos of his equipment setup at a recent reception. Are unsightly cords and wires hanging out in plain sight? **(Photo 1)** If he uses lights, do they fit with your reception location's décor, or do they look like the kind of lights you'd see at a high school prom? **(Photo 2)** Keep in mind that the DJ's equipment setups may end up in the backdrop of many of the photos taken at your reception. Some DJs have gone so far as to put covers on their speakers and draping or using a façade in front of their equipment setups to make them more aesthetically pleasing. Bob Carpenter, a wedding entertainer in Greenville, Rhode Island, is using the new BOSE L1 Cylindrical Radiator System, but can you see it in the photo? **(Photo 4)** Andy Austin, a wedding entertainer in Dallas/Fort Worth, Texas, has a façade that can be customized to match the color of the bridesmaid's dresses or the table linens. **(Photo 5)** You'll be investing a lot of time and money creating the colors and décor that will dress up your reception. Make sure your DJ's equipment setup will fit into that setting as well.

What does he think is more important — professional equipment or unique talent?

This question is specifically designed to help you identify if the DJ believes his real value is found in the amount and quality of his sound equipment or in his uniquely specialized talents. Many DJs suffer from the misconception that what they bring (their gear) is more important or has more value than what they can do (their talent). This can be plainly seen when their Web sites feature prominent pictures of their speakers, microphones, light shows, mixers, amps, and equipment setups. Best of all is a Web site with pictures of DJs holding their microphones in front of their speakers and their light shows. **(Photo 3)**

Did your caterer show you photos of their chafing dishes? Did your photographer show you their collection of lenses? When you see photos of sound equipment being emphasized, you are likely dealing with a DJ who sees his own talents as secondary to his equipment. He may be choosing to buy newer and better equipment instead of investing in techniques and opportunities for improving his talents. But if great gear is all that's required to make yours "The Best Wedding Reception...Ever!", then you could just rent the necessary equipment and have your friends provide your entertainment.

A truly professional DJ should know that unique talent is the most important factor in creating an unforgettably fun celebration.

Will he charge extra for additional speakers and/or cordless microphones?

A DJ should make sure that he has the necessary tools to properly deliver his service and performance. Speakers and cordless microphones should be standard. A DJ who isn't already charging a professional fee to begin with will be more likely to tack on extra fees for the basic tools he should already have to get the job done right. There are situations where special requests, such as a large lighting setup, will require a greater number of staff to set up and run. In such special cases, it is reasonable to pay extra for the additional equipment and services.

How many microphones will he provide for your wedding ceremony?

This may seem like an unimportant question at first glance, until you experience a wedding ceremony where the officiant can be clearly heard, but the bride and groom cannot. The overall purpose of a wedding is to celebrate your lifelong commitment of marriage. But if your guests can't hear the two of you exchanging your vows, then they will feel left out in the middle of your ceremony. At a recent ceremony that I attended as a guest, the officiant was given a lavaliere microphone (a clip-on lapel mic) by the location, but there was no mic provided for the bride and groom. As they began sharing their personally written vows, even their parents

The iPod Wedding

Apple's popular portable digital music player, the iPod, has been making the news quite a bit lately when it comes to weddings. The common theme between the news and feature stories were brides and grooms who didn't want a "cheesy DJ" to ruin their wedding day and preferred to be able to maintain complete control over their music selections.

For the financially strapped wedding reception, an iPod may be a highly viable option. But the one factor most of these stories have not covered was the actual end result of using an iPod to provide the music for a ceremony and/ or reception celebration.

In her August 13, 2006, article for the *Chicago Tribune*, titled "The Do-It-Yourself Wedding Soundtrack," Angel Rozas reported on an iPod wedding she had attended: "The ceremony was halted midway through when the 'iPod attendant,' as he was listed in the wedding program, could not figure out how to stop a song from playing. Steve (the groom), who was holding his bride's hand, turned to make the international 'Turn it off!' sign, sliding his finger across his throat. Another friend jumped up to help. No luck. With 70 pairs of eyes on him, the groom left the bride and walked over to fix the iPod. It wasn't the only glitch. The start of the wedding had been delayed until someone could figure out how to cue the right song for the bride to march down the aisle. During the reception, the iPod's downloads were playing at uneven volumes, forcing another friend to run back and forth to the music table to adjust the sound." When asked why they opted to use an iPod for their ceremony and reception, the groom in the story said, "Why do we want to pay some dopey deejay $3,000 to press play on a CD changer when we can spend that money on something more important than that?"

A truly unforgettable celebration requires an individual with the talent and skill to not only play the right music at just the right moment, but also the ability to guide and direct your celebration while keeping the guests informed and involved.

It is almost impossible for an iPod to create an entertaining reception on its own. If your wedding reception requires more than subtle background music, consider the other entertainment options outlined in this chapter.

in the front row couldn't hear them. Your words and your voices will be of the utmost importance at that particular moment. It is reasonable to insist that the DJ provide two lavaliere/lapel microphones for your ceremony, or at least a handheld cordless microphone that the officiant can use to let your guests hear your vows.

What kind of backup systems does he have for his PA equipment?

If your DJ has just one CD deck, one computer, one mixer, or one amplifier and any one of these components suffers a malfunction in the middle of your reception, your celebration could take a dramatic turn for the worse. Professional entertainers know from experience that redundant systems are needed to ensure an uninterrupted performance at your reception.

At a recent reception, my DJ mixer began to malfunction during my initial sound-check. I was able to swap out the defective mixer and replace it with a backup mixer well before any serious problems could have occurred. If I had not had my backup mixer on site, my reception performance could have suffered severely.

Remember, backup PA equipment is a backup only if your DJ actually brings it along.

THE MASTER OF CEREMONIES

Since the beginning of wedding celebrations, music and entertainment have undoubtedly played a major role in creating fun-filled, memorable moments. Bands were the only option for musical entertainment until mobile disc jockeys came on the scene in the early 1970s. At the time, most DJs delivered the same service as bands … they just played music. In an effort to provide more value to their wedding clients while creating more successfully entertaining receptions, some DJs began offering to additionally serve as the master of ceremonies (MC). Soon, many DJs began promising to offer the same level and quality of services, with little to no training, as MCs, for "half the price." The generally accepted idea was that being a DJ and MC was easy and fun and just about anyone could do it with very little time, effort, or money invested.

Regardless of whether you are hiring a band or a DJ to provide the entertainment at your wedding reception, the additional services provided by a qualified master of ceremonies will only help to ensure a smoother-flowing experience that is more personalized and memorable for you and your guests. Here are some important benefits to consider regarding the role of a master of ceremonies:

• The master of ceremonies will keep your guests appropriately informed and involved.

- The master of ceremonies will plan and direct your celebration so it will flow seamlessly.

- The master of ceremonies will keep the attention focused on you instead of stealing the spotlight.

There are at least four additional services that a MC should provide for his brides and grooms. In order to create a not-soon-to-be-forgotten entertainment experience, a qualified MC should provide comprehensive personalization, creative involvement, and event direction. On top of that, a professional MC will be prepared to serve as a talented spokesperson.

What is comprehensive personalization?

Comprehensive personalization includes helping you plan your ceremony and/or reception agenda with a timeline of events and a list of participants who will be involved or may need to be introduced.

An MC will help you to create your ceremony and/or reception agenda from the entertainment perspective. During your initial consultation and planning process, he should listen to your ideas while offering his experienced advice to ensure that your schedule of events will not only be uniquely yours, but will also be thoroughly entertaining for your family and friends. He should help you select the traditional events that fit your style and then organize them into a script that will keep your celebration moving along at a pace of your choosing. He should help you create the lineup order for your wedding party's grand entrance while making sure he can confidently pronounce any difficult names. The goal for the MC should be to make sure the agenda, the flow, and the special moments in your reception have been completely personalized to fit your unique style, taste, and personality.

What is creative involvement?

Creative involvement includes providing you with ideas that are designed to make your guests feel more involved. It may also include the development of ideas that have been custom-crafted for your unique situation.

An MC should have a wide variety of suggestions for creating appropriate guest involvement in a reception. These ideas may include, but are not limited to centerpiece giveaways, sing-along activities, buffet release, and personalizing your wedding party's grand entrance. These ideas will be explored in much greater detail in Part 3: "Adding Your Personal Style."

An MC should be more than willing to help you create memorable moments with your guests. To see a clear example of how a surprise entrée choice was turned into a moment that involved the guests in a simple, yet entertaining way, turn to page 31 and read the spotlight segment on Peter and Nichole's reception.

No one wants to feel left out at a wedding reception. When your guests are allowed, or better yet invited, to become active participants throughout your reception celebration, they will relax, they will make new friends, they will have more fun, they will be more inclined to dance when the time comes, and they will stay longer. An MC should advise you about selecting the right amount of involvement for your group so that everyone has an enjoyable time without ever feeling over-involved.

What is event direction?

Event direction is the art and science of keeping your agenda on track while keeping your guests entertained. The science part includes double-checking the important details behind the scenes (such as making sure the cake knife is at the cake table) and communicating with your reception team members (i.e., the caterer, photographer, videographer, etc.,) to make sure everything and everyone is ready before moving onto the next activity on your agenda. The art part includes "reading your crowd" to make sure they are not getting bored or restless while making sure they never see the science part taking place (announcing for someone to go find

Presenting the **Wedding Entertainment Director**

Because the wedding entertainment industry has remained completely unregulated, anyone can go into business and instantly declare he is a professional wedding entertainer or MC with little or no training. In an effort to create a verifiable brand of professionally qualified wedding entertainers and MCs who have been proven to be the best of the best, the trademarked term Wedding Entertainment Director was developed. Wedding Entertainment Directors provide entertainment and MC services that have been verified to meet and surpass a measurable, professional caliber. To create this professional standard and verification process, the Wedding Entertainment Directors Guild was formed in May 2007. The guild utilizes a rigorous application process to verify that each and every member is a proven professional with a minimum of five years of experience in wedding entertainment or a minimum of 200 wedding reception performances. To see just how strenuous and thorough the application process is, or to look for a current W.E.D. Guild–qualified Wedding Entertainment Director in your area, visit their Web site (http://WEDGuild.com).

the cake knife over the PA system).

An MC will consistently go out of his way to communicate in advance with your ceremony and/or reception team members, including your ceremony officiant, wedding coordinator, caterer, photographer, and videographer. A qualified MC knows from experience that your team of vendors will work together better and your reception will flow more smoothly when everyone is working off the same script. If your photographer wants to take a group photo with all of the guests, an MC will work with you and your photographer to place the group photo into your agenda where it will do the most good and the least harm.

An MC should always use a preventative wedding reception direction checklist to manage the details behind the scenes at your ceremony and/or reception that could turn into possible problems later on. Like a director of a movie, an MC should recognize that each important person and prop needs to be in place and ready at the right time for your reception's events to move as smoothly as the action on a movie screen. If the photographer is out of the room, an MC will make sure he is aware of the next special event that is about to occur, so he will have plenty of time to return and get ready for the next important photograph. If champagne for the toast has not yet been poured, an MC will alert the catering staff and then wait until everyone has been served before beginning the formal toasts. An MC should always be more than happy to show you the reception direction checklist he uses to keep a celebration moving along smoothly.

An MC should always insist on becoming familiar with your chosen location for your ceremony and reception. MCs know how important room layout can be for the overall success of an entertaining reception. If 70 percent of the guests are seated around the corner from the head table, for example, the toasts will need to take place in a spot that is easily visible to all the guests. Extra amplification may also be needed to make sure those toasts can be heard around that corner.

Some of these services may already be provided by your wedding coordinator, so there may be some overlap with the details that are managed by an MC. This subject will be covered in greater detail in the next chapter. It should be stated, however, that an MC will likely still insist on double-checking the details that can directly impact the pacing and flow of your reception.

How will a talented spokesperson make your reception better?

A talented spokesperson will utilize his proven public speaking skills, along with any additional entertainment training and experience he may have, to communicate with your guests in a manner that captures their attention, keeps them properly informed, and encourages them to have an enjoyable time.

Professional MCs should have invested a lot of time improving their abilities as public speakers while additionally expanding their capabilities as entertainers. Many have taken a class or a workshop on acting, singing, dancing, or even stand-up comedy. Some have even worked in television and/or radio. They have learned from experience that the confidence to speak well in front of a live audience comes from ongoing practice, rehearsal, and training.

An MC will also recognize that beyond just making announcements, everything he says verbally and nonverbally will reflect directly on you. This fact alone compels him to get to know you on a personal level. Don't be surprised if your MC wants to know everything he can about your families, the history of your relationship, your likes and dislikes in both music and humor, what you do for a living, etc. By knowing you well, an MC will know the right thing to say in the right moment.

Here are some important questions to consider before selecting someone to serve as your master of ceremonies.

What training has he taken to develop his skills as an MC?

Many opportunities are available for developing the skills required to be a polished MC. One can join a local club of Toastmasters International (http://www.Toastmasters.org) or take a class on public speaking. Acting, voice-over, and comedy workshops can also be quite helpful. The point is, someone who is serious about properly filling the role of MC at your reception will invest the necessary time to become truly exceptional. Only amateurs "wing" it. Ask the MCs you interview to make sample announcements as an audition. Are they personalized or compelling? Do you want to hear this person continue to talk? Remember, your MC is your spokesperson at your reception.

What is his entertainment background?

Being a good MC, fulfilling the role of properly representing you as your spokesperson, will require someone with unique talent and skills. Many bands and DJs have limited themselves to musical training and experience, or DJ training and experience alone. Although they may play music well or mix music well, their ability to guide, direct, and motivate your guests using announcements that are concise, confident, and effective may be somewhat limited. However, if they have a wide base of entertainment experience and training, their ability to clearly communicate in a polished manner that fits your expectations may be much more likely. A qualified MC will have taken classes or workshops in acting, singing, public speaking, stand-up comedy, and more. They may even have a background in radio, theater, television, or voice-over. Be sure to ask your prospective MC for a description of his entertainment background and allow him to share with you how those experiences have made him a better MC, spokesperson, and wedding entertainer.

How can he assist you in planning the agenda for your ceremony and/or reception?

An MC should be more than happy to help you create a detailed agenda. MCs have learned through experience that a well-planned reception will always turn out much better than one that is disorganized. Some DJs or bands may tell you that they actually prefer to "wing it" when it comes to your reception's agenda. What they are really telling you is that they don't have the time or the desire to help you plan your agenda. No quality MC ever just "wings it."

I learned this lesson first-hand when I took a workshop in stand-up comedy and then performed onstage at The Improv in Irvine, California. The best comedians look like they are spontaneously making up funny jokes while they are onstage. The reality is they have often spent weeks, months, or years developing their unique routines and writing and rewriting their best material. By being well prepared, they are able to deliver a performance that appears completely fresh and entertaining. The amount of time an MC is willing to invest in helping you create a detailed agenda will have a direct effect on how smoothly your reception will flow.

An MC will most likely offer and require at least one face-to-face meeting. Some will even offer two or more meetings as needed. By investing time with you to discuss your preferences and desires, he will be able to help you create a very personalized agenda for your ceremony and/or reception. He should provide you with forms or a list of questions to help you think about the type of reception events you want to do and don't want to do. He will be more than willing to offer helpful advice about the pacing and flow of your reception agenda.

Does he have a reception direction checklist?

If a band or DJ tells you that they regularly "coordinate" the details at their receptions, ask to see a copy of their direction checklists (see sample checklist, page 86) that they use to double-check details behind the scenes of their ceremonies and receptions. If they are unable to produce such checklists, perhaps they are relying on a mental checklist or perhaps they are not really managing these details at all. Such a checklist should include things like: making sure the cake knife and cake server are on the cake table, making sure the parents are alerted discreetly before they will be needed for their special dances, or verifying that the bride has her garter on before it's time to begin the garter removal and toss. When details like these are managed effectively behind the scenes, the result will be a reception that flows very smoothly. This will only happen when someone is making sure the props and/or players are in the right places at the right time. Unfortunately, the "coordination" that is offered by some wedding bands and many average DJs is usually more of a reactive approach to problem-solving. This means they will "react" when something goes wrong and then try to solve it, rather than being proactive by trying to prevent such problems from occurring in the first place. A qualified MC should always be proactive and will likely spot possible glitches before they become problems.

At one reception where I was an MC, I was double-checking some last minute details with the bride. When I asked her if she had her garter on for later, she realized that her garter had been left at home. She was understandably upset. I told her not to worry as I always carry a back-up garter for just such emergencies. Later that night, the garter removal and toss went off just as planned. The guests never knew that an unfortunate situation had been avoided thanks to careful preparation and direction.

Can you see uncut video footage of the MC performing at a reception?
Requesting to see uncut video footage is vitally important. Uncut video footage will show you everything and is one of the most reliable ways to verify the true qualifications and skills of an MC. A well-qualified MC will often review uncut video footage of his own performances for the purpose of self-critique and personal improvement. When you watch his footage, watch the way he makes announcements. Is he making announcements in a polished, professional, and personalized manner? Listen closely. Does he refer to the bride and groom by name? Does he announce the special dances in a uniquely personalized way, or does it sound like every other wedding announcement you've ever heard? Is he using repetitive phrases like "Ladies and Gentlemen" or "At this time…"? Is he making eye contact with the guests, or does he appear nervous or unsure while speaking? Is he rambling endlessly instead of making announcements that are concise and effective? Is he saying anything that you would consider inappropriate? I once heard a story about a wedding DJ making jokes about his three ex-wives on the microphone at a reception. I wrote it off as fiction until I found a real DJ bragging online about making such tasteless comments as part of his cake cutting announcements.

Remember, the person you choose to MC your special day will not only be making announcements, but will also be serving as your spokesperson. Choose the person that you feel will be able to represent you to your guests in the best manner possible.

Choosing Your Wedding Officiant

While the officiant you choose to perform your wedding ceremony is not officially a part of the reception, the officiant will often set the tone for the rest of your wedding festivities. If you've ever sat through a ceremony that was officiated without feeling or emotion, you already know how vital the role played by your officiant will be in making your ceremony meaningful and memorable.

These questions may help you to identify the best officiant for your needs:

Can you see the officiant's set ceremony?

Most wedding officiants have a set ceremony outline, or variations thereof, that they follow. The officiant should be more than happy to share this set ceremony with you so you can discuss the order and your personal expectations in great detail. If not, that should be cause for concern. After all, how will you know that the officiant won't say or do something during your ceremony that would not fit your desires, unless you can see it and discuss it ahead of time? If the officiant offers you a wide variety of set ceremonies from which to choose, you are most likely in good hands.

Can you make personalized adjustments to the officiant's set ceremony?

If not, you might have to settle for what this officiant "always does" instead of getting the personalization you were expecting. Some couples like the traditional pronouncement of "man and wife" while others might find it offensive. Some couples may prefer vows that end with "as long as we both shall live" over vows that end with "until death do us part." Don't be afraid to raise these issues with your officiant.

Can you see video footage of the officiant performing a wedding ceremony?

This will enable you to see and hear first-hand how the officiant speaks and carries himself when officiating a wedding ceremony. Does he sound happy for the bride and groom, or does he sound like he has said these same words so often that the words have lost all meaning and value? Watch the officiant's expressions and body language.

Will the officiant be able to attend your rehearsal?

Many professional officiants are not always available to attend the rehearsal. If having your officiant at your rehearsal is important to you, be sure to ask him before you make your final selection. Keep in mind that while some officiants may be willing to attend your rehearsal, they may charge an additional fee to do so.

CHAPTER 7
NOMINATING THE BEST DIRECTOR
Appointing the Best Person to Guide and Direct Your Reception

*W*hen a movie receives rave reviews, its success is usually attributed to the director's artistic vision and efforts. The director often reworks the script to make sure the dialogue and scenes will flow naturally. The director also makes sure the various props are in place and the actors know their blocking and their cues. Finally, the director oversees the filming of each scene to make sure the proper actions and emotions have been created and captured in a manner that keeps the overall plot moving along effectively.

Good entertainment always requires someone to fill the role of the director, whether the entertainment in question is an exciting fast-paced movie or an unforgettably fun wedding reception. But far too often at wedding receptions, these duties are overlooked or are taken on by someone without the best qualifications for the role. If you want your reception to be a fun, smooth-flowing, and entertaining celebration, it is vital that you select someone who is well qualified to serve as the director. This decision, more than any other, can have the greatest impact on whether your guests get bored and restless, or whether they enjoy themselves so much that they'll find themselves commenting that yours was truly "The Best Wedding Reception…Ever!"

A GOOD DIRECTOR ALWAYS HAS A PLAN

An entertaining wedding reception won't just fall into place all by itself. Whomever you choose as your reception director should be able to help you create an agenda that will not only incorporate your personal style, but will also maintain the proper pacing and flow required to keep your guests interested and involved. If a movie director can tell that the script is too slow or too wordy, he will make changes to speed up the dialogue. In a similar manner, the director of your

reception will offer advice and suggestions to ensure that your chosen formalities are scheduled into your agenda in the most effective way possible. This subject will be covered in greater detail in Part 2: "Creating Your Timeline."

The methods for creating your agenda may differ from director to director, but it is vital that you include your entertainment vendor in this process. Some locations may prefer to have someone on their staff serve as your director. But more often than not, the agenda created by the location will be one that best suits the needs of their staff or the personal preferences of the location's owner, rather than being designed to create a smooth-flowing entertainment experience.

Some wedding coordinators may prefer to create your agenda timeline without any input from your entertainment vendors. If their experience includes creating highly entertaining receptions, then their input may be all you need. However, if their strengths are more focused on the décor than on keeping your guests engaged in your celebration, you may be allowing a "producer" to serve as your "director" and the results could be very disappointing. Some DJs and bands will work with you to create an agenda that will not only be fun, but will also keep your reception events moving along with very little downtime. A professional MC who is acting as your reception director will insist on meeting with you in advance to create an agenda that will result in a smooth-flowing, personalized reception.

In a recent phone conversation with a less than professional wedding coordinator, I was told point blank that being present at an agenda planning meeting was "not my place." It was made very clear to me by this coordinator that my role was to plan the music choices only, and she would inform me about the reception agenda two weeks prior to the wedding date. If my role was to "just play the music" then I would be in agreement with her. But as the MC as well as the reception director, I had a vital role to play in ensuring that my client's reception celebration would be as fun as possible. It became apparent that we were at an impasse.

The input your entertainment vendors have to offer regarding your agenda should be given a high priority, if not top priority. They are the ones who make your party work. But if they are forced to use a script that isn't entertaining, or filled with downtime, their job will not only be much more difficult, but the quality of the results they will be able to deliver (guests enjoying themselves, more guests dancing, etc.,) may be hampered as well. Your location staff wouldn't dream of telling your photographer not to use their flash to capture your special moments. Your coordinator would never tell your cake maker to leave off the frosting. Yet it is all too common to find locations and coordinators who will tell your entertainment vendors to carry out an agenda that may have serious flaws.

If creating an entertaining reception celebration is high on your list of priorities, then it is imperative that whomever you select to serve as your director should be someone who is highly qualified to create an agenda that will not only flow smoothly, but also be thoroughly entertaining.

DIRECTING A RECEPTION REQUIRES ENTERTAINMENT EXPERIENCE

There is a good reason why many movie actors have been able to transition successfully into becoming movie directors. Due to their experience in creating entertaining moments in front of the camera, they realized that they had a well-developed skill set for creating such moments from behind the camera as well. It should also be noted that the best directors are known not only for their innovative ideas, but also for creating movies that are powerfully emotional, incredibly memorable, and captivatingly entertaining. Likewise, the director you choose should be able to help you create an emotional, memorable, and entertaining reception.

A director's primary role is to create a movie, a stage play, or a wedding reception that will be creative and consistently entertaining. For this reason alone, it makes very little sense to hand over these duties to someone who doesn't have either

entertainment experience or a deep understanding about creating effectively entertaining moments.

If you have ever been a guest at a wedding reception that just dragged along and you had no idea what would happen next, chances are that no one was selected to serve as the director, or that whomever was entrusted with the director's duties lacked the entertainment experience and knowledge to keep the reception agenda moving at a steady pace.

Let's explore the definition of the titles of the vendors who will guide your reception:

Coordinator

Somebody bringing together different elements; somebody responsible for organizing diverse parts of an enterprise or groups into a coherent or efficient whole.

Producer

A person responsible for the financial and administrative aspects of a stage, film, television, or radio production; the person who exercises general supervision of a production and is responsible chiefly for raising money, hiring technicians and artists, etc., required to stage a play, make a motion picture, or the like.

Master of Ceremonies

A person who directs the entertainment at a party, dinner, nightclub, radio or television broadcast, or the like, acting as host and introducing the speakers or performers.

Director

The person responsible for the interpretive aspects of a stage, film, or television production; the person who supervises the integration of all the elements, such as acting, staging, and lighting, required to realize the writer's conception.

Notice how the definitions for coordinator and producer are very similar, while there are striking differences between the roles of a producer and a director. It is also quite remarkable that the definition given for master of ceremonies utilizes the phrase "directs the entertainment."

Unfortunately, many entertainers who are chosen to fill the duties of the MC are unprepared to actually direct the pacing and flow of their wedding receptions. Similarly, most wedding coordinators have been trained only to function as

producers and are lacking in the entertainment experience needed to effectively direct the pacing and flow of their events as well. As always, there are exceptions in both cases. Ultimately, however, the best director for the overall pacing and flow of your reception is the person with the most entertainment experience. That person may be a wedding coordinator or the person you have selected to serve as your MC. However, if both have

strong entertainment backgrounds, it would be best to nominate your MC to serve as the director of your reception's overall pacing and flow — in other words, to be your reception director.

If your wedding coordinator recognizes that your MC has well-established skills and talents, they should both be able to work together as a team to ensure that your reception is entirely successful. However, if your wedding coordinator is more concerned with being "in charge" of your MC, unnecessary power struggles could result in mishaps, conflicts, and unneeded stress.

A DIRECTOR IS PREPARED TO PREVENT PROBLEMS

On a movie set, the director has taken precautions to make sure the lighting and audio settings are perfect before attempting to film a given scene. In a similar manner, the director at your reception will take precautions to make sure your vendors are ready and in place before starting something as important as your first dance.

I have heard stories of DJs announcing the first dance when the bride and groom were not even in the room; and the MC who announced the cake cutting without first notifying the photographer; and the band leader who introduced the formal toasts before the catering staff had been able to serve the champagne. Each of these examples could have been prevented by a qualified director using a wedding reception direction checklist to ensure that the other vendors, the guests of honor, and the necessary props were all in their proper places before beginning the next scheduled event on the agenda.

Whether your wedding coordinator or your MC will be entrusted with directing your reception, be sure to ask for a copy of their wedding reception direction checklist. A highly qualified reception director will gladly show you the list of details he manages behind the scenes to prevent problems from occurring. If he cannot share one with you, perhaps he will just be winging it as your director.

SAMPLE WEDDING RECEPTION DIRECTION CHECKLIST

PRE-ARRIVAL:	
Compare notes with catering manager/wedding coordinator	
Clarify grand entrance path to head table	
Check cake table for utensils, plates, napkins, and throw bouquet	
ARRIVAL OF THE WEDDING PARTY:	
Alert catering staff to pour for the toast	
Line up wedding party for grand entrance	
Confirm best man's toast with best man	
Brief best man on microphone technique	
THE MEAL:	
Announce buffet guidelines	
Does the bride have the garter on already?	
Does the bride have her purse for the money dance?	
Alert parents about upcoming special dances	
Give catering staff an ETA for cake cutting	

The Value of Using a Professional Wedding Entertainment Director

The best reasons for nominating a Wedding Entertainment Director to serve as the director of your reception are contained in the three words of their title.

"Wedding": A Wedding Entertainment Director specializes in weddings. Directing corporate functions, a birthday party, or even a school dance requires entirely different skills. Someone who has a deep understanding of the etiquette, traditions, and personalization that can be required to create a truly unforgettable wedding reception celebration will always treat each wedding reception with his very best personal service. Whereas a director who "specializes" (and I use that term loosely) in a wide variety of events may be more inclined to treat his wedding receptions as just another "gig."

"Entertainment": A Wedding Entertainment Director is an experienced and talented entertainer who will know exactly how to make your wedding reception as entertaining as possible. A director whose focus and background encompasses producing the overall décor may be able to create a visually stimulating setting, but the pacing, flow, and total entertainment experience may still come up short.

"Director": A Wedding Entertainment Director not only knows how to direct an entertaining reception, but has also proven that his skill levels as a director are truly professional. Some who claim to direct their receptions are merely solving problems after they occur, instead of preventing them from ever becoming problems in the first place. Some of them will "direct" your special moments by interrupting them or even talking over them on their microphone. But a Wedding Entertainment Director will always strive to do most of his directing from behind the scenes.

To learn more about the comprehensive services that can be provided by a Wedding Entertainment Director, visit the Web site (http://WeddingEntertainment Director.com). To find a fully qualified Wedding Entertainment Director near you, visit the membership listing on the Wedding Entertainment Directors Guild Web site, (http://www.WEDGuild.com).

PART 2 *Creating Your Timeline*

Writing a Reception Plan That Will Flow Smoothly

Great entertainment cannot happen without a great script. Too often the fun moments of a wedding reception can become just "to do" items on a checklist. However, if your definition of a successful reception calls for the fun moments to be the focus and the priority, this section will help you to create a timeline that will flow smoothly while keeping your guests consistently entertained.

CHAPTER 8

PICKING THE PACE

Deciding on a Relaxed or Fast-Paced Schedule

. . . .

ome wedding receptions feel hurried and even frantic, while others may feel like they'll never end. There are many factors to consider when choosing the pacing of your reception. Your personal preferences about pacing might be thwarted by your location's time constraints, your guest count, or even your photographer's schedule. This chapter will help you determine what kind of pacing will fit best for your celebration. We will also examine some of the common roadblocks that could complicate the pacing you are hoping to achieve.

. . . .

THE RELAXED RECEPTION

When describing a relaxed reception schedule, these are some of the images that come to mind: a formal, elegant reception with a five-course meal that is served over two hours; a large celebration with food stations that remain open for most of the evening; an extended cocktail hour with tray-passed hors d'oeuvres followed by a reception filled with more dancing and fewer of the traditional festivities; guests who have plenty of time to connect with and congratulate the bride and groom.

These images all evoke feelings of a fun celebration that is laid-back and stress-free. Such a relaxed schedule can take place over four to eight hours or even longer. Creating this relaxed pace in a four-hour time frame, however, may require combining or omitting some of the traditional festivities. However, with a longer time frame, creating such a relaxed schedule will not only be much easier to achieve, but there will also be less pressure to combine or cut any of the traditional festivities.

The relaxed reception can have some drawbacks, however. If your schedule becomes too relaxed, your guests may get bored or restless. If your MC is not adept at "reading the crowd" to see the onset of boredom, he may neglect to take

steps to pick up the pace when and if it may be needed. If he is not prepared to properly keep your guests informed about what is coming up next, they might begin to feel left out of your celebration. These kinds of feelings can lead to your guests thinking about leaving sooner than you might want.

THE FAST-PACED RECEPTION

Here are some of the images that come to mind with a fast-paced reception schedule: a lively, energetic reception with something new happening from one minute to the next; dancing that starts early and ends early, while you still have a large crowd on the dance floor; a quick buffet dinner or just heavy appetizers and a chocolate fountain; a celebration that starts off fun, stays fun, and ends on a high note.

Such a fast-paced schedule could take place over four to five hours, but probably shouldn't last much longer. Some of the traditional festivities may need to be cut and/or combined, especially if having more time for dancing is a high priority.

The fast-paced reception also has drawbacks. If the schedule becomes too rushed, your guests can easily begin to feel overwhelmed and even worn out. If your MC is more accustomed to a relaxed schedule, the faster pace may impact his ability to prevent problems from occurring. Your MC may mistakenly become too energetic, too quickly, in an effort to get your guests involved and can easily turn off your guests.

THE BLENDED RECEPTION

A blended reception schedule takes the best aspects of both previous examples and combines them into a schedule that may start off relaxed while slowly building into a energetic celebration. Imagine your guests enjoying a laid-back cocktail hour and then, as the reception begins, the pacing rises along a growing energy curve that will culminate in a fully packed dance floor with everyone feeling involved.

The blended reception schedule can work for a four-hour reception, but you may need to consider cutting and/or combining some of the traditional festivities, especially if having more time for open dancing is a high priority.

Drawbacks of the blended reception schedule include: If your schedule builds energy too slowly, guests could bore more quickly. If your schedule builds energy too quickly, your guests may get worn out too soon, especially if your time frame is longer than six hours. If your MC is not familiar with creating an energy curve that builds, he may find this pacing difficult to manage effectively. If your MC is too subdued for too long, the energy might not build when needed. If your MC is too energetic too early, your guests may get turned off.

SCHEDULING CONSIDERATIONS

The pacing for your reception is completely your choice, but there are some key factors that may limit or even constrain what is possible. The more information you arm yourself with in advance — such as planning for venue time constraints, guest counts, and vendor availability — the more likely you will be able to create the pacing that will fit your style and desires.

Possible location time constraints
If your location allows only four to five hours for your reception, creating a relaxed reception may be a bit challenging. However, if your location will give you an unlimited time frame (eight hours or more), you should be free to

Be Prepared to Make Changes if Needed

If the pacing you have designed is not working for some reason, you may need to pick up the pace or even slow it down to ensure that your guests will continue to have an enjoyable time. This subject will be covered in greater detail in Chapter 11: "Preparing a 'Plan B'."

create just about any kind of pacing you'd like. As I already discussed in Chapter 4, learning the time constraints of your chosen location should play an important role in helping you select the right location for a well-paced reception.

Some locations have time constraints because they schedule more than one event/ reception per day. Others may have time constraints due to local ordinances concerning noise levels late at night, while some may have limitations on how late they can serve alcohol. Some venues will host your ceremony, cocktail hour, and reception, but the room for your reception may only be ready at a set time, due to cleanup constraints from whatever took place in that room previously. This means that even if your ceremony, cocktail hour, and reception are scheduled for the entire facility from 5:00 to 11:00 p.m., but the reception room is not ready until 7:00 p.m., you will have only four hours for your traditional festivities, meal, and dancing. Such limitations can understandably have a dramatic impact on the desired pacing of your celebration.

Some locations may tell you that the cut-off time for music and dancing is 11:00 p.m., when in fact that is the deadline by which all of your guests need to be gone and any personal clean-up must be completed. Some facilities with such a deadline may require that the music and dancing end no later than 10:30 p.m. If information like this is not discussed in advance, it can create some real frustrations, especially if you and your guests have been hoping to dance a little longer, and the celebration is forced to stop sooner than expected.

Guest count considerations

If you want a fast-paced schedule, but you have more than 300 guests, it will become very cumbersome to move quickly from one event to the next. Delays can be caused simply by the difficulty created in locating vendors and any VIPs that are needed in the large crowd before beginning the next event on your agenda.

Working with vendors' schedules

The time you have scheduled with your other vendors can impact the overall pacing of your reception. If your reception will last until 11:00 p.m., but you only have your photographer contracted until 9:00 p.m., you may have to rush through some of your festivities a little faster than desired to ensure that those moments are captured before your photographer leaves. If you and your photographer go outdoors for sunset photos, for instance, your absence could have a dramatic effect on the pacing of your reception.

Whenever possible, secure vendors who will be present for your entire celebration from the beginning until the end. The pressure caused by making changes to your reception's schedule to accommodate a vendor whose time is almost up can cause big problems for the desired pacing you were hoping to achieve.

Make sure you are fully aware how much your vendors, including your entertainment, will expect to be paid for going overtime, past their contractual obligations. Some vendors may give you a price break on added hours when you first book with them, but charge much more for added hours if they are tacked on at the event itself. Some vendors offer unlimited time as part of their services.

ANDERSON & MAGGIE

OCTOBER 28, 2006
SILVERADO CANYON, CALIFORNIA

The Dancing Never Stopped

Anderson and Maggie wanted their guests to enjoy a relaxed, laid-back reception that would just naturally turn into a huge dancing party. They chose food stations instead of a formal meal. Their 350 guests were encouraged to eat whenever they were hungry, dance whenever they were ready, and visit with Anderson and Maggie whenever they were nearby. They passed on most of the traditional events and even tossed their bouquet and garter during the open dancing.

* PRIVATE CAKE CUTTING

Rather than stop the dancing for the formal cake cutting, Anderson and Maggie opted to cut their cake "under the radar" with no fanfare while their photographer and videographer captured their private dessert exchange. Then the guests were all treated to their own individual cupcakes!

RECEPTION AGENDA

5:00–6:15
Cocktail Hour

6:15
Grand Entrance
"Numb/Encore"
by Jay-Z & Linkin Park

6:30
First Dance
"An Angel Above Me"
by Tommy Tokioka

6:35
Toasts

6:50–9:00
Food Stations for Meal

7:10–10:00
Open Dancing

8:00
Maggie's Dedication
"Making Memories Of Us"
by Keith Urban

8:45
Bouquet & Garter Toss
"Girls Just Want To Have Fun"
by Cyndi Lauper
"She's A Beauty"
by The Tubes
"Legs"
by ZZ Top
"Everybody Wants You"
by Billy Squier

9:00
* Private Cake Cutting

10:00
Last Dance
"You'll Accomp'ny Me"
by Bob Seger
& The Silver Bullet Band

10:00–10:30
After Party

CHAPTER 9
CHOOSING THE EVENTS
Deciding Which Formalities Will Fit Your Celebration

ome wedding receptions are very traditional with all of the events and festivities that have been done for decades or even centuries. Others have been crafted with very few or none of the traditional activities, sometimes incorporating new ideas for creating memorable moments. There is no right or wrong any more when it comes to choosing the traditions and activities that that will be a part of your celebration. Just because some events may be "traditional" and you may feel that they are expected doesn't mean you're required to include them. This is your wedding reception. You should do everything that you'd like to do and nothing that you wouldn't. Don't be afraid to say "No." Likewise, don't be afraid to get creative and come up with a completely new idea.

In this chapter, I will discuss the options for both traditional and modern events, while encouraging you to follow your heart and select the ones that are truly important to you. In Part 3: "Adding Your Personal Style," I will discuss each of these events in greater detail, including creative ways they can be personalized.

THE TRADITIONAL EVENTS

These are the events that probably took place when your parents got married and maybe even when their parents got married. Some of these traditions may appeal to you, and some others may not. Some may feel like requirements. You may feel pressured by certain family members to do one or more of them even though you personally don't care for them. Here is a list of questions to help you select which ones will work for you and which you'd prefer not to do:

Will you have a cocktail hour?
If so, think about what kinds of appetizers and drinks you will provide for your

guests. If background music is an option, think about your preferences in selections.

Will you have a grand entrance?

If so, think about who will be introduced, in what order, and by whom. Will your parents be introduced? How about the ushers or your wedding party? Will there be music? Which selections will create the effect you want to create?

Will you have any formal toasts?

If so, will they be given by the best man, the father of the bride, or both? In what order will the toasts be given? Will the groom speak last? Will anyone else be expected to give a toast? Will they be told in advance so they can be prepared? Will a cordless, handheld microphone be provided so everyone can hear the toasts?

Will someone be asked to give a blessing for the meal?

Depending on your religious background and that of your family, this may be something that you want to do. If so, who will you choose to give the blessing? Will he or she be asked in advance? Will a cordless, handheld microphone be provided so everyone can hear the blessing? Will the catering staff know to wait before serving the meal or opening the buffet or food stations?

Will you provide a meal?

If so, will it be a formal sit-down meal or a buffet? If it will be a sit-down meal, how

many courses will be served? Will there be dancing between the courses? If it will be a buffet, will it feature one or more lines? Will there be various food stations? How long will it take the catering staff to serve all of your guests?

Will you have special dances?

Will the two of you have a first dance? Will the bride share a special dance with her father? Will the groom share a special dance with his mother? Will the two of you share in a special dance with your parents?

If so, have you selected a song for each special dance? Will you be slow dancing or doing a choreographed dance? Will the song be known to both of you, or will one of you be surprising the other with the selection? If the song feels too long, would you like it to fade out early or perhaps create a shorter, edited version? When in the reception would you like to do each of these dances?

Will you share a special dance with your wedding party?

If so, have you selected a song? Will this be a slow or a fast dance? Do you want your wedding party members to dance as couples, or can they dance with their spouses and/or dates? When would you like to do your wedding party dance?

Will you have a cake cutting?

If so, will you be providing your own cake knife and server? When would you like to cut your cake? Are there any music selections you'd like played during the cake cutting? Do you want your guests to be invited to gather around and take pictures? Will you be feeding each other nicely, or will you be smashing cake into each other's face? Will there be charms baked into the cake? Will there also be a groom's cake? Who will slice and serve the cake?

Will you have a money dance/dollar dance?

If so, will both of you be participating? Do you have a purse for the money dance? When would you like to do the dance? Will your best man and maid of honor assist you by regulating the lines? Will you be dancing to slow, moderate, or fast songs?

KARL & LORI

OCTOBER 29, 2005
IRVINE, CALIFORNIA

Nobody Danced?

It's quite true…nobody danced at Karl and Lori's reception. Since neither they, nor their families, would be interested in dancing, they chose to forgo the dance floor and pass on the special dances. However, creating a celebration filled with laughter was a high priority, so we planned several unique events to keep their guests entertained.

* NEWLYWED QUIZ

We placed Karl and Lori in chairs, seated back to back, and then we quizzed them about how well they really knew each other (for example, "Which one of you is the better kisser?"). They signaled their answers by holding up a groom's shoe or a bride's shoe, while unable to see the other's response. When they both heartily agreed about which of them had the "crazy family," their guests let out a roar of laughter.

RECEPTION AGENDA

1:00–2:10
Drinks & Appetizers
Vocal Jazz Background Music Mix

2:10
Grand Entrance
Wedding Party Themes
"Father Of The Bride Theme"
"Rocky Theme"
"Green Acres Theme"
"Hawaii Five-O Theme"
"The Imperial March"
Love Story Theme
"What A Wonderful World"
by Roger Williams
Bride & Groom's Theme
"Beautiful Day" by U2

2:20
Formal Toasts

2:30
Dinner
*Background Music Mix feat.
Glenn Miller, Chris Botti &
Nat King Cole*
Salad Course
Kissing Couples Drawing
Longevity Spotlight
*"You're Nobody 'Til
Somebody Loves You"
by Dean Martin*

3:00
Entrée Course
Centerpiece Giveaway
Words of Wisdom
RSVP Spotlight
* Newlywed Quiz

3:45
Cake Cutting
"Sweet Happy Life" by Peggy Lee
"Jaws Theme" by John Williams

3:55
Chocolate Fountain

4:30
Last Song
*"Wonderful Tonight"
by Eric Clapton*
Finale Clip
"The Muppet Show Closing Theme"

Will you have a bouquet toss?

If so, what music selections would you like during the toss? Will your florist be providing a "throw bouquet" for your bouquet toss? When would you like to do the bouquet toss? How many single women will want to participate?

Will you have a garter removal and toss?

If so, what music selections would you like during it? When would you like to do your garter removal and toss? How many single men will be ready and willing to participate?

Will you have a last dance?

If so, have you selected a song? Will you choose a slow or a fast song? Will the song be known to both of you, or will one of you be surprising the other with the selection? When would you like to do your last dance? Will your guests be asked to share the last dance with you?

Will you have a big sendoff?

If so, will your guests need any special instructions for participating? Will you be providing them with birdseed, flower petals, sparklers, glow ropes, etc.?

THE MODERN EVENTS

These are the events that have become common or even popular within the last 50 years. Some may appeal to you, and some others may not. Here is a list of questions to help you select which ones you would like to do:

Will you do any centerpiece giveaway activities?

If so, when? Do you want the giveaway activity to build up energy, or would you prefer to keep things low-key? Will any special props be needed? Will the entire centerpiece be taken home, or just the floral arrangement itself?

Will you have a video montage/slideshow?

If so, how long will the entire presentation last? Who will produce it? Will an audio track be included with it? Will the proper connections be available to patch the audio feed into the entertainment's sound system? Who will be providing the projector, power extension cables, and screen for the video montage/slideshow? Where will it be set up? When would you like to do the show? Will there be time to test it fully before your reception begins?

Will you have a longevity/anniversary spotlight?

If so, is there a particular couple, married for a considerable length of time, who you want to spotlight? How many married couples will want to participate? When will you do it? Do you want to spotlight them at their tables or during a special dance? If this will be during a dance, do you have a song selected?

Will you have a sorority song?

If so, how many sorority sisters will be willing to participate? Will the sorority song be presented privately in a different room or in front of the guests? Where and when would you like to do the song?

COMBINING SOME EVENTS CAN HELP SAVE TIME

If your time frame for your reception will be limited, or if you just want to create some extra time for open dancing, then combining some of your special events may be a helpful solution. Here are some questions to help you determine if combining some events might be a good fit for you:

Would you like to combine your first dance and grand entrance?

If you are from the East Coast, this might not even be an option. We'll cover regional differences in agendas in greater detail in Chapter 10. Would you like to get your first dance out of the way as soon as possible, or would you prefer to wait until after the meal? Will the dance floor be cleared for dancing when you make your grand entrance, or will it be occupied by the buffet tables or your cake table?

Will you combine the father/daughter and mother/son dances?

If so, have you selected a song that is more moderate and less focused on either the bride's father or the groom's mother? Will you both begin at the same time, or will the bride and her father go first, while the groom joins in with his mother halfway through? When would you like to do these dances?

Will you combine the parents and wedding party dances?

If so, have you selected a song that is more moderate and less focused on either the parents or the wedding party? Will everyone join in together from the beginning, or will you both begin with your parents and then invite the wedding party to join in halfway through? Will this be a slow dance or a fast dance? Do you want your wedding party members to dance as couples, or can they dance with their spouses and/or dates? When would you like to do these dances?

CHAPTER 10

SCHEDULING FOR SUCCESS
Drafting a Script That Will Keep Your Guests Entertained

. . . .

A wedding reception that feels like it's dragging probably has a poorly planned agenda. If the script for your celebration is not designed with the overall entertainment value in mind, what may have initially looked like lots of fun on paper could instead wind up being rather dull. In this chapter, I will explore the art and science of creating a reception agenda that will keep your guests thoroughly involved and entertained. You will learn how to create a lineup for your events that not only will flow smoothly, but also will keep your guests entertained with the pacing and personal style you have been working so hard to generate. Don't be afraid to try something new, while keeping in mind that your overall goal is to make sure that everyone has a fantastic time.

. . . .

PUTTING YOUR DESIRED PACING TOGETHER WITH YOUR EVENTS

Once you've deciding on the kind of pacing as well as the events you want to include in your reception, it's time to put all the pieces together into a format that is both well structured and smooth-flowing. If your desired pacing is fast, then your events may need to be scheduled closer together with very little downtime between them. If you want a more relaxed pace, you might want to spread some of your events out and give yourself more time to meet and greet with your guests or even dance.

If you want the pacing to start off relaxed while slowly building into an energetic party, you might put some of the lower energy events early in the schedule while saving some of the higher energy events for later.

Don't overload your guests

One common mistake is packing too many events into the agenda so that the guests will never be bored. This can result in an agenda that is top-heavy with activities, leaving your guests feeling overwhelmed. Too much of even a good thing is still too much. More isn't always better. As you read through the creative ideas in Part 3: "Adding Your Personal Style," just hold onto only the best ideas, instead of all of the good ideas. Your MC should be willing to advise you if your agenda is becoming too full.

Be discerning with your location's suggested agenda

Many locations have a pretty good idea about the kinds of agendas that have worked out well at their venues. But some locations can get downright pushy about your order of events and try to require that you follow their suggested timeline, even if it is not an optimal schedule for an entertaining reception. These types of locations are, thankfully, rather rare. If the location does a large number of events, it may have developed certain patterns for reception agendas that work best for its staff. But these preferred patterns may not take into consideration whether the guests will be consistently entertained or will feel bored and restless. I once saw a catering manager turn up the house lights an hour before the dancing was scheduled to finish so the guests would begin leaving, causing the reception to end prematurely. Cleaning up early was more important to the venue than hosting a memorable celebration. If you are not aware that the location will assert more control over the order of your events than you'd prefer, you may find yourself in a few unpleasant confrontations.

Typically, a wedding reception will begin with a cocktail hour as the guests are arriving or are waiting for the bride and groom to finish up with their formal photos. When the wedding party arrives, there may be a grand entrance followed by formal toasts, or the first dance, or even just the meal itself. Sometimes it may be best to move to the cake cutting right after the grand entrance.

One of my brides followed her Vietnamese traditions by changing her dress for a traditional toasting that is done at each table during the meal. Then, after the meal, she changed back into her formal bridal gown. With the limited festivities they had selected and the dress changes factored in, we decided to do their grand entrance, followed by the first dance and then the cake cutting, which then led into their formal toasts.

Formal toasts

The formal toasts can be done before the meal, after the meal, or even before the cake cutting. Whichever time you choose, keep your regional expectations in mind and think about setting it at a time when you will have most, if not all, of your guests' undivided attention.

Formalities during the meal

If someone will be saying a blessing for the meal, this will immediately follow the formal toasts (if they are scheduled before the meal).

In some regions, the meal is usually a buffet with an informal receiving line that funnels into the buffet line. Keep in mind that you and your parents (and whoever else is in the receiving line) will be eating after all of your guests have gone through the line.

In many cases, the bride and groom (and often the wedding party) are served first so they can mingle and visit with their guests at their tables. Always remember to take some time to eat so you don't run out of steam yourselves.

Centerpiece giveaway

If you will be doing a centerpiece giveaway activity, the type of meal you are serving may determine where and when it should happen. For a buffet, the activity should be scheduled to begin only after the buffet line has cleared out. I once saw video footage of a band doing a popular centerpiece giveaway activity that involved all of the guests at their tables, but a third of the guests were in the buffet line and were completely left out. For a sit-down meal, a good time might be right after the salad course has been served. If you will have food stations spread throughout the room,

Sample Reception Agendas

New York City Agenda
Cocktail Hour
Grand Entrance
First Dance
Open Dancing
Salad Course
Father/Daughter Dance
Mother/Son Dance
Open Dancing
Entrée Course
Formal Toasts
Longevity Dance
Open Dancing
Cake Cutting
Bouquet & Garter Tosses
Open Dancing
Last Dance

Chicago Agenda
Cocktail Hour
Grand Entrance
Cake Cutting
Formal Toasts
Salad & Entrée Courses
First Dance
Father/Daughter Dance
Mother/Son Dance
Longevity Dance
Open Dancing
Bouquet & Garter Tosses
Open Dancing
Last Dance

Southern California Agenda
Cocktail Hour
Grand Entrance
Formal Toasts
Salad & Entrée Courses
First Dance
Father/Daughter Dance
Mother/Son Dance
Longevity Dance
Open Dancing
Cake Cutting
Bouquet & Garter Tosses
Open Dancing
Last Dance

it may be best to do the centerpiece giveaway activity just before the guests are invited to begin leaving their seats to help themselves to the food. Timing can make a big difference, while also creating some fun energy.

Video montage/slideshow

A video montage/slideshow can be scheduled at several times. The first consideration will be the lighting. If your location will be flooded with daylight (an outdoor location or an indoor facility with large windows), the timing of your slideshow will need to be measured against the time that the sun is expected to set. The video montage/slideshow can be a precursor to your grand entrance or after the cake cutting. But one of the best times for a video montage/slideshow is just as the meal is beginning to end. At this point, your guests are still seated and they will be ready to enjoy the presentation.

Special dances

Taking your regional agenda expectations into account, you may want to kick things off with your first dance right after your grand entrance or save it until the end of the meal. When your special dances are grouped together at the end of the meal, too many of them in a row may start to make your guests feel restless. If your regional agenda calls for dancing between the courses of the meal, kicking off each new segment of open dancing with another special dance can spread out those dances.

In my region (Southern California), it is typical to save the special dances until the end of the meal. But I have seen couples successfully kick off their first dance right after the grand entrance and even do the father/daughter and/or mother/son dances while the guests are eating their salads. At a fantastic wedding reception in New Jersey, the guests joined the dancing right after the bride and groom's grand entrance and first dance. After 20 minutes of energetic dancing, everyone was seated for the formal toast and the salad course. Next was the father/daughter dance, leading into another 20 minutes of lively dancing. Then everyone resumed their seats once again for the entrée course, during which time we did the centerpiece giveaway activity. After that, we started the mother/son dance, which segued into the next fun-filled 20 minutes of dancing. Finally, the dancing stopped one last time for the cake cutting and the dessert course. A couple who was celebrating their tenth anniversary led off the final segment of dancing with a slow song dedication that just happened to have been their first dance song. Trying to make that happen in Southern California would be difficult, to say the least, due to regional norms. (Coincidentally, I had a Southern California couple who opted to use this exact model for their reception's agenda. With some careful planning and a concise, advanced explanation of the timeline for the guests, we were able to create a truly memorable celebration with plenty of dancing between each of the courses.)

Cake cutting

As mentioned earlier, your cake cutting can occur before the meal, after the meal, or even a little later. Taking your regional considerations into account, this still comes down to your own preferences. Some will say, "Cut the cake early so your makeup will still look good and the two of you won't be sweating in your photos." Others will say, "Cut the cake as the meal is ending. Serve it as dessert." And some will even say to cut the cake as late as possible because "guests often wait to leave until after the cake cutting." The truth is, the guests will leave after the cake cutting, but only if they are not being entertained, don't feel included, or are not enjoying themselves.

I often recommend scheduling the cake cutting to take place about 45 minutes after the meal has ended so the guests can get involved in some fun dancing before

Regional Differences in Agendas Need to Be Considered

When planning your agenda, examine what's most common to your particular region. People in different regions have different expectations as to how a reception will flow. If you create an agenda that is completely unfamiliar in your area, your guests will be much more likely to feel things are not going smoothly. This doesn't mean it is impossible to try something new; it's just wise to be aware of the norms before attempting to create something that is drastically different.

In New Jersey, for example, the guests will expect to begin dancing right after the grand entrance and will continue dancing between each of the meal courses, sitting only when each course is served. In Southern California, the guests expect to begin dancing only after the meal has been completely served and cleared. In parts of Wisconsin, the bride and groom commonly enter the reception with little or no fanfare, cut their cake without the guests even noticing, and then are seated at their head table to prepare for the meal. In Sacramento, the bride and groom, along with their wedding party, usually make a big splash with their grand entrance, and the cake is cut right at the end of the meal.

As you can clearly see from these examples and the sample agendas on page 105, the difference between agendas in various regions can be quite dramatic.

they start feeling restless. Granted, this may work in conjunction with my regional norms and might not be appropriate in other regions. However, one thing that I have noticed over the years is that when the cake is served right at the end of the meal, it tends to go uneaten to a large degree, as most of the guests may still feel rather full. But when it is served 45 minutes after the meal, following a good calorie-burning workout on the dance floor, a larger percentage of guests will eat most, if not all, of their cake.

Money dance/dollar dance

I cover several ways to present this event in much greater detail in Chapter 20. As for the timing, here are a few key points to consider. If your money dance/dollar dance will be set to slow or moderate music selections, it will be more of a low energy moment. If you have a large guest count (200 or more), your dance could stretch out and last longer than you want. If your music selections for this dance will be more upbeat, you might be able to do it during your open dancing. But if the low energy example is more in line with your plans, I would recommend scheduling it for just after the cake cutting. This way all of your guests will have something to do. They can participate in your money dance/dollar dance or they can take a moment to enjoy some cake. Scheduling a slower money dance/dollar dance during or following your open dancing can cause problems, as the sharp dip in energy may lead your guests to perceive that the celebration is waning.

Bouquet and garter toss

When and where should you schedule your bouquet and garter toss events? Some may say to do the bouquet and garter toss right at the end of the meal, maybe after the cake cutting and just before the special dances. Others may say to save them until much later in your celebration. But if the number of guests begins to drop, you could be left with fewer participants than you might have wanted. Keep in mind that when done well, the bouquet and garter toss can really create good energy. So it might be wise to place them after a lower energy event, like your cake cutting or the money dance/dollar dance, to get your guests ready to resume more open dancing. Another idea would be to pass on the traditional method that only the single people can participate, and instead do the bouquet and garter toss during the open dancing with no stipulations on who is eligible. Read Chapter 21 for more suggestions.

Open dancing

Once again, your regional norms may play a large role in determining when, where, and how much open dancing you will be able to put into your scripted timeline. If your region is primarily familiar with dancing from the very beginning and between each of the meal courses, attempting to make your guests wait until the end of the meal might be a challenging endeavor. Likewise, attempting to create fun dancing from the beginning in a region like mine, where the guests don't expect to get started until well after the meal, could prove nearly impossible. Discussing these issues with your reception director during your planning process will be very helpful. Just because your desires may not fit with your regional norms doesn't mean that you can't or shouldn't ever attempt to try something new. The agenda for Anderson and Maggie's reception (page 95) was completely foreign for the regional expectations held by their guests. But with some careful planning, it not only worked — it was a huge success.

The ending

Finally, we need to consider when it will be appropriate to call it a night and do your last dance. If you plan to stay at your reception until the last dance (instead of sneaking out early), keep in mind that the ending can be one of the most memorable moments your guests will experience. I will cover this subject in greater detail in Chapters 24 and 25. Simply put, your reception can last until the wee hours of the morning with your closest friends who really like to party. Or you can plan for an ending that involves most of your guests in the last dance and a big sendoff. Unless your location has a rigid ending time with a short time frame, the timing for ending is entirely up to you. Don't get trapped into thinking that your reception has to last as long as you have access to the location. Be open to the idea of wrapping up early if doing so will create the best possible ending for your celebration.

Another option suggested by Randy Bartlett, a nationally known DJ trainer and Wedding Entertainment Director based in Sacramento, California, is to "try staging an 'early ending' with a finale song (including a sendoff if you'd like) and then announcing the beginning of 'the after party' where the music can be geared more towards the younger guests who will be more likely to stay later into the night. This will give the older guests, who might be inclined to leave early, the feeling that they have participated in the entire reception. And it can also create a more memorable ending for the majority of your guests while still allowing you to extend the dancing late into the night."

Smoking Can Be Hazardous to Your Celebration

Suffice it to say, if you or your new spouse has to take cigarette breaks on a regular basis, the pacing and flow of your reception could be impacted. Limiting your cigarette breaks or wearing a nicotine patch might help. Always tell your MC where you will be before leaving to take any cigarette breaks.

CHAPTER 11
PREPARING A "PLAN B"

Planning a Strategy for Navigating Unexpected Circumstances

*A*s John Lennon wrote, "Life is what happens to you while you're busy making other plans." This proverb also holds true for creating successful reception celebrations. Even the best-laid plans can get foiled when "life happens." Luckily for us, we can predict some of the mishaps that may occur, so we can prepare some "Plan B" solutions before they are needed. It is said that airline pilots are not really trained to fly planes, because the planes practically fly themselves these days. Instead, pilots are put through rigorous training so that when, and if, "life happens," they are prepared. Captain Sully's miraculous water landing in the Hudson River is a great example. Applying this same methodology to your plans will not only help you feel more prepared, but will also help relieve any added stress caused when, or if, a predictable mishap occurs. Let's get to work.

BLAME IT ON THE RAIN

One couple I had the pleasure of working with made a cute video about the planning that had gone into their wedding and reception. We all got a good laugh during the scene where Jenny was researching online the weather conditions for their date and region. Even though her research said rain was only a remote possibility, we all remembered how the rain had indeed come. What could have spelled certain doom for most outdoor receptions was averted thanks to the great Plan B provided by their unique location. Their ceremony and reception had been set outdoors with no covering from the elements. But fortunately, their location also had a large indoor reception hall available. When a slight drizzle began falling towards the end of the meal, we quickly moved to Plan B and everyone moved inside within 15 minutes, just in time to start the dancing. Their celebration went overtime by an hour and everyone said they were having the time of their lives.

Inclement weather can put a real damper on a reception celebration, so it is vital to have a Plan B. Some outdoor facilities may have tent vendors on call for last minute changes due to poor weather conditions.

But undesirable weather is not just limited to rain or snow. Extremely high or low temperatures can also cause unexpected problems. If your reception hall has no air conditioning, and your summer wedding date experiences record levels of heat, your guests may begin to feel like they are melting. Large table umbrellas for shade along with cooling fans and handheld paper fans can give your guests some relief from overwhelming heat. An outdoor celebration with unexpectedly cold conditions can cause big problems. Plan ahead. Find out if your location can provide portable space heaters, or even a fully enclosed tent with forced air heating, should you need them.

UNEXPECTED DELAYS

Delays of some sort can have a detrimental effect on your reception's success, but many of them can be prevented. However, it is still wise to prepare a Plan B for your agenda. It may be necessary to move around some of your events in order to create more energy sooner or to ensure that the desired amount of time for open dancing will still be achievable. I have seen weddings delayed because the photographer took twice as long as expected with the post-ceremony formal photos, or because the

location was unable to "turn the room" fast enough when a prior event ran late, or an important family member or wedding party member was late. When "life happens" in instances like these, your Plan B solutions should give you peace of mind.

One beautiful Saturday afternoon in August, I ran into an unexpected delay when the guests began arriving at the reception location — on a lovely harbor beach in Southern California — almost a full hour after they were expected. The ceremony had taken place about 20 miles away, but it seemed that everyone in Orange County had decided to go to that beach that particular day. This caused the guests to be held up in massive traffic delays. Needless to say, I began to get worried because the wedding party was going to be about 45 minutes behind their guests, because of photos. The buffet was already set up, the food was ready, and the guests of honor were running even later than their guests. Having the location scheduled from noon to 4:00 p.m., with no possibility of going overtime, I knew a solid Plan B was the only way we could save this reception. When Kevin and Athena finally arrived at 2:00, they were understandably upset since they now had less than two hours to turn their reception into a fun celebration. I had already taken the liberty of inviting their guests to begin eating much earlier. My advice for Kevin and Athena was for them to pass on eating so we could get through their reception events more quickly. We still had 45 minutes left for open dancing after doing a grand entrance, formal toasts, all the special dances, cake cutting, and the bouquet and garter tosses. The pacing was certainly rushed, but it was still a fun reception.

NOT FEELING TOO WELL?

Health issues, although thankfully rare, can still bring a rousing celebration to a screeching halt. I personally know a DJ who has been the entertainer at three separate receptions where an invited guest suffered a heart attack and died.

Although such dire circumstances have thankfully never occurred at one of my receptions, I am fully aware that "life happens."

I have, however, personally experienced a few non-tragic health issues with guests at weddings over the years and have learned some simple Plan B methods for continuing the celebration.

At one wedding reception, the groom's mother had a serious allergic reaction to something she ate. An ambulance came to treat her and she regained the ability to breathe more normally. But in the meantime, the bride and groom, surrounded by about a third of their guests, were outside tending to her. The rest of the guests inside were slowly becoming aware of what was happening and were getting restless. I moved into Plan B and changed the music to something mellow while letting the guests know that we were going to be delayed and asking them to be patient until this crisis could be resolved. I also invited those who felt so inclined to offer up a prayer or two for the groom's mother and her speedy recovery. When she was finally stabilized, the paramedics took her to the hospital just to be safe, and the bride and groom and their guests slowly filtered back into the reception. The groom was understandably distressed, but he was surrounded by his closest friends and family members who were there to support him. The celebration resumed, they cut their cake, and they even danced with their guests for a short time before wrapping up with a last dance. Choosing to be candid with the guests not only helped keep them from leaving early, but it also empowered them to shower the bride and groom with positive support.

During your planning process, discuss with your reception director or MC any concerns you may have about the mishaps that might occur at your reception. Most things that can go wrong at a wedding reception are somewhat predictable. Don't wait until the moment hits and get caught off-guard. Make your plans as complete as possible by formulating your Plan B solutions so you can be confident that inclement weather, unexpected delays, and minor health concerns won't cause your plans to be ruined.

CHAPTER 12

INFORMING YOUR TEAM

Keeping Your Vendors on the Same Page

. . . .

*Y*our wedding vendors should be the all-stars who will do whatever they can to make your reception a fantastic and entertaining success. That means, of course, they will all need to be kept updated in advance with the latest information from the scripted timelines for your ceremony and/or reception. They will also need to keep communicating with each other throughout your celebration, especially if there are any last minute changes. The ideal person to act as your team leader and main informer during the reception is your reception director (the role discussed in detail in Chapter 7: Nominating the Best Director). Keeping your team on the same page will go a long way toward creating a fun reception that will flow smoothly, while preventing conflicts or miscommunication between your vendors. In this chapter, we will discuss how this dialogue can be most effectively accomplished.*

. . . .

PHONE, FAX, OR E-MAIL?

In today's technologically advanced world, staying in constant contact has become faster and much more convenient. You will undoubtedly be collecting contact information for your various wedding vendors so you can reach them quickly whenever the need arises. You'll want their phone numbers (including cell phones), fax numbers, and e-mail addresses. Be sure to share that contact information list with your other vendors, especially those who will be the most involved in the actual production of your reception. These may include your ceremony officiant, location manager, catering manager, wedding coordinator, entertainment vendors, photographer, videographer, and your reception director.

Find out in advance the name and personal contact information of the actual person who will be representing each vendor on your wedding day. You don't want any last minute surprises. At a wedding rehearsal a few years ago, I

watched as a bride was introduced for the first time to the location coordinator who had been put in charge of overseeing her ceremony and reception. She was understandably apprehensive.

WHO'S GOING TO MAKE THE CALLS BEFORE YOUR WEDDING DAY?

If you have a professional wedding coordinator assisting with your planning, he may be the person you want contacting the rest of your team on your behalf about the ceremony and/or reception agendas in advance of the big day. If you have chosen someone to be your reception director, that person should be eager to make these calls to keep the rest of your team fully up to speed. However, if you will be managing your planning details, it is still vitally important for your entire team of vendors to receive advance information from you regarding your scripted timelines.

KEEPING EVERYONE IN THE LOOP ON YOUR WEDDING DAY

During your reception, it will be very important for your team of vendors to be kept informed about which event will be coming up next and any changes that may take place as well. You'll be too busy to do this yourself. That's one reason why it is so important to select vendors who are "team players," meaning they're accustomed to keeping each other updated. A reception director (whether your wedding coordinator, your MC, or someone else who is filling this role) will be prepared to keep your other vendors in the loop before starting any new events, and they will certainly take the time to communicate throughout your celebration with your vendors.

Lay down the simple ground rule that your reception director should be directly notified by your other vendors before they leave the room for any reason. If the bride and groom are ready for their first dance, but the videographer cannot be located in a timely manner, the first dance may get delayed. If the photographer wants to take the bride and groom outside for sunset photos, but your reception director is not notified or given an ETA on their return, he may be left wondering where they are.

I once had a location coordinator who got upset with me for starting the cake cutting without her. The bride had insisted on starting the cake cutting a little sooner than either of us had anticipated. And so, after making several fruitless attempts to find the location coordinator, I informed the rest of the team and then made several announcements that we were about to do the cake cutting. I was hoping that the coordinator would hear my announcements, wherever she was, and

MICHAEL & ELIZABETH

DECEMBER 19, 2009
RIVERSIDE, CALIFORNIA

Their Moment in the Spotlight

Michael and Elizabeth chose a very unique location for their wedding reception. Elizabeth's father was the stage manager for their local university's theater. The guests were invited to sit at tables set on the stage. Using the theater's lighting, the stage went completely dark except for a large circle of light shining down on Michael and Elizabeth during their first dance.

* WEDDING PARTY DANCE

Michael and Elizabeth decided to use their wedding party dance to kick off their open dancing. Instead of choosing a typical slow song, they opted instead for a fast, upbeat dancing song. Their wedding party members formed a "soul train," with couples dancing their way down the center of the dance floor. Soon, they were inviting the guests to come join them and the dancing was off to a great start.

RECEPTION AGENDA

6:00
Grand Entrance
"I Gotta Feeling"
by Black Eyed Peas

6:10
Toasts

6:25–7:15
Dinner

7:15–7:30
The Special Dances
First Dance
"Love Is Not A Fight"
by Warren Barfield

Father/Daughter Dance
"Ragtime Theme"
by Randy Newman

Mother/Son Dance
"What A Wonderful World"
by Louis Armstrong

* Wedding Party Dance
"Don't Stop The Music"
by Rihanna

7:30–7:55
Open Dancing

7:55
Cake Cutting
"When I'm Sixty-Four"
by The Beatles
"That's Amoré"
by Dean Martin

8:10
Honeymoon Dance

8:25
Bouquet & Garter Toss
"Single Ladies (Put A Ring On It)"
by Beyoncé
"The Wanderer" by Dion
"At Last" by Etta James
"NFL Theme" by Scott Schreer

8:35–10:00
Open Dancing

10:00
Last Dance
"(I've Had) The Time Of My Life"
by Jennifer Warnes & Bill Medley

be ready to assist them as needed. As my luck would have it, she came running in from the kitchen just after the bride and groom had begun to cut their cake. If she had followed the simple ground rule for effective team communication, I would have known where to find her and an uncomfortable misunderstanding could have been prevented.

GETTING LOST IN THE CROWD

If your guest count is rather large, it may become difficult for your reception director to locate the rest of your vendors when needed. Encourage all the team members to make regular eye contact with each other and especially with your reception director. In a large crowd, sometimes just being able to make eye contact and exchange simple hand signals from across the room is all that's needed to ensure that the whole team is ready for the next important event.

Andy Austin, a wedding entertainer in the Dallas/Fort Worth area, came up with an ingeniously simple way to keep his fellow wedding vendors, and even his VIPs, informed in overly large crowds. He uses mini text pagers controlled by his computer system so he can send out a text message that might say, "Best man's toast in 10 minutes!" Your entire team of vendors (and even the best man) would be instantly notified on their own vibrating mini pagers, provided to them before the reception began.

Adding Your Personal Style

Putting Your Fingerprints on Every Page of Your Reception Plan

The most unique part of any reception is the bride and the groom. Almost all receptions have a cake and flowers and decorations and tuxedos and dresses and food and linens and photographs. But your guests won't be attending to see any of those things. Your guests will be there to see you, to congratulate you, to celebrate with you, and to laugh and cry with you. This section will feature the memorable moments that your guests will be talking about for years to come.

Important Disclaimers for
the Entertainment Ideas Presented in Part 3:

- Some of the ideas presented in the following chapters may not be a good fit for you. Use the ideas that fit your personal style.

- Don't be afraid to come up with your own creative ideas.

- It is vital that you discuss with your MC how you would like these events to be presented and when you would like to do them.

- Make sure you clearly spell out what you consider appropriate and inappropriate.

- Each MC's level of skill and talent for presenting these events can vary greatly.

- Ask for video footage to see how your MC has presented these ideas in the past.

- Make sure your MC knows how to pronounce any names that may be challenging.

- Make sure your MC fully understands how to deliver these ideas properly so they won't be presented poorly.

The ideas in this section will range from the simple to the highly complex and will be scored as follows:

* Very Basic
These are ideas that you can implement without any assistance.

** Basic
These are ideas that you could pull off with practice and some training.

*** Intermediate
These are ideas that will require help from someone with some specialized skills and/or talents.

**** Advanced
These are ideas that will require help from someone with proven skills and/or talents.

***** Very Advanced
These are ideas that will require finding someone with the very best quality skills and/or talents.

CHAPTER 13

THE WEDDING CEREMONY

Your wedding ceremony will be attended by your closest friends and family. Ever since they first heard the news of your engagement, they have been looking forward to watching as the two of you become husband and wife. The reception that follows will be a celebration of the lifelong commitment you will be making. Your choices for your ceremony can and will be the precursor that lets your guests know what kind of reception celebration they are about to experience. In an effort to make their ceremonies more personal and entertaining, more than half of my clients hire me to help with their wedding ceremony in addition to their reception. Whether your choices will lean toward traditional or nontraditional ideas, you should feel free to put your personal touches into each and every aspect of your wedding ceremony.

HERE COMES THE BRIDE *

One of the first questions that will come to mind relates to your musical selections. Will you be choosing traditional, classical selections or nontraditional music for your processionals and recessional? Or will you use a little of both? If your theme will be traditional, keep in mind that there are many different versions of the traditional, classical pieces such as the ever-popular "Canon in D Major" by Johann Pachelbel. That piece sounds quite different on a harp or a piano, or even when it is performed by an orchestra. If nontraditional selections will be more your style, feel free to get creative and do what will fit best for you.

At a ceremony a few years ago, the bride and groom picked out their own nontraditional musical selections. The mothers were escorted forward and seated to "Maybe I'm Amazed" by Jem. The officiant, the groom, and his groomsmen all came strolling in while "Little Green Bag" by The George Baker Selection was playing. (This song is the opening theme from one of the groom's favorite movies, *Reservoir Dogs.*) Then the bridesmaids came forward while a specially edited loop of "Bittersweet Symphony" by The Verve was played. Finally, the bride was escorted down the aisle by her father to the ballad, "Angel Standing By" by Jewel. When the ceremony ended and the officiant introduced them as husband and wife, they exited down the aisle to "Ring Of Fire" by Social Distortion.

THE GROOM'S ENTRANCE SONG *

As just suggested, personalizing the music that plays when the groom comes in with the officiant and his best man and/or groomsmen can be a fun way to start your ceremony. One groom, a big fan of Johnny Cash, chose "I Walk The Line." Another groom chose the theme song from the TV show, *The Dukes of Hazzard* by Waylon Jennings. The guests began to cheer as he and his groomsmen entered during the song's lyrics that started with "Just a good ol' boys…" At a New Year's Eve wedding in 2009, the groom made his entrance before the ceremony to the song "Under Pressure" by Queen featuring David Bowie. When the guests recognized the song and saw the groom biting his lower lip nervously, they began laughing and cheering for him.

BRIDE'S SURPRISE VOICE-OVER MESSAGE DURING THE PROCESSIONAL *****

Larry Williams, a Wedding Entertainment Director from Reno, suggested this breathtaking idea: "As the bride and her father make their way to the start of the aisle, they pause for just a moment. During the rehearsal, the father is told that this momentary pause would give the photographer a chance to get a great photo. But then the music level dips down slightly and the bride's prerecorded voice can be heard telling her father how much it means to her that he is about to walk her down the aisle. The look on his face and the emotion she is expressing in her message will create a memory every single guest will not soon forget. Capturing and mixing this recording to create the desired effect will not be easy. The person playing the prerecorded music and message and the officiant must be made aware of this surprise so they can help ensure that is properly staged."

WRITE YOUR OWN VOWS *

In addition to, or in place of, the vows your officiant will be using during the ceremony, you could write and recite your own vows to each other. It can be something as simple as a list of the things you truly love about each other, or it can be heartfelt promises that have been written in your own words, incorporating your

unique style, your personality, your emotions, and maybe even your sense of humor. Make sure your voices will be properly amplified so your guests will be able to enjoy this moment with you.

Bettie-Jeanne Rivard-Darby, an officiant who specializes in creating personalized ceremonies for her clients in Connecticut, says, "Some of my clients have opted to incorporate a creative twist into writing their vows. One client requested vows that were written in the style of Dr. Seuss. Another client requested vows that were written in the unusual speaking style of the character Yoda, from *Star Wars*. This added level of personalization made their ceremonies more unique, more fun, and certainly more memorable."

HAVE SOMEONE GIVE A SPECIAL READING *

This can be a great way to involve someone special who was not included in your wedding party. Whether you select a passage from the Bible, a poem, or even a few lines of Shakespeare, this option can add a more personalized feeling to your ceremony. Be sure to ask for an additional microphone so your guests will be able to hear your reader.

AN EXCHANGE OF LOVE LETTERS ****

At one wedding ceremony, the bride and groom wrote personal love letters to each other, which they asked their best man and maid of honor to read aloud on their behalf. With 300 guests in attendance, it was very important to make sure everyone could hear the letters as they were being read aloud. Wireless lavaliere microphones were put on both the best man and the maid of honor so they could remain right next to the bride and groom as they read their respective letters, and everyone was able to hear them clearly as a result.

HAVE SOMEONE SING A SPECIAL SONG ✳✳✳

If you have a close friend or family member who loves to sing, and can sing well,

this can be a great way to let him play an important role in your ceremony. Make sure he has his own music (an accompaniment track), and be sure to request an additional microphone so your guests will be able to hear. The singer might want to rehearse before the guests arrive; rehearsal arrangements should be discussed with your entertainment vendors in advance.

At a wedding ceremony a few years ago, the bride's cousin had been asked to sing "You And Me" by Lifehouse in the middle of the ceremony. He sang so well, everyone had goose bumps. Only later did I learn that he had been a top-12 contestant on *American Idol*.

THE BINDING/"HAND FASTING" CEREMONY ✳✳✳

Your officiant uses a small rope to "bind" your hands together while you make a series of promises to one another. After each promise of love is made, more rope is entwined around your hands until you have both been symbolically secured to one another.

LIGHT A UNITY CANDLE ✳✳

Use a unity candle to create a symbolic act representing your new union as husband and wife. You can even ask your mothers to get involved by having them light the two outer candles you will use later to light the unity candle. If your ceremony will take place outdoors, be sure to check out the wind conditions and consider providing hurricane covers so the candles will stay lit. If it is not already provided, you will need to bring a lighter of some kind. Having small votive candles already lit on the table can create a much nicer look than using lighters to ignite the outer candles. This might be a good moment for a special song to be played in the background.

THE SAND CEREMONY **

This symbolic act may be perfect for outdoor settings that are too windy for candles. Fill two different containers (vases, seashells, antique bottles, etc.) with two different colors of sand. The bride and groom will pour their separate containers into one larger container (preferably one that is made of clear glass), creating a mixed pattern. Additional containers can be provided for children and/or stepchildren so they can be invited to participate as well. Consider playing a special song in the background.

PRESENT PROMISES TO STEPCHILDREN **

If either of you has children from a previous relationship, take a moment to express a separate commitment to your new stepchildren in the form of personalized promises and/or presenting them with a commemorative item (such as a medallion, bracelet, etc.). This will make your future stepchildren feel included in a very special way. A special song can be played in the background. If you would like your guests to enjoy this moment with you, make sure your voices will be properly amplified. Or arrange to have the microphones muted if you would prefer to keep this special moment private.

BLESSING THE RINGS ****

With a long piece of satin ribbon that's quickly strewn down each row of guests, starting from one side of the aisle and coming back down the other, pass your rings down the ribbon so that each person can touch them briefly in a symbolic act of blessing your rings. This idea is a little complicated, but it will allow every guest to be an active participant in your ceremony. This might be a good moment for a special song to be played in the background.

THE SURPRISE RING BEARER ***

When your officiant asks for the rings, the best man will act caught off guard and begin patting down his pockets. Suddenly, a fanfare of music begins to play as a special friend, who as of yet had not been included, comes down the aisle, presenting the rings on a pillow for all to see.

PRESENT ROSES TO YOUR MOTHERS *

Take a moment during your ceremony to present your mothers with a long-stemmed rose (or a small bouquet of flowers) in a symbolic gesture of your gratitude. You could play a special song in the background.

HONORING THE DEARLY DEPARTED *

Take a moment during your ceremony to honor any departed loved ones, especially recently deceased parents and/or grandparents. This can be done with the lighting of commemorative candles, reserving an empty chair in the front row for them, or placing a rose or a bouquet of flowers on a chair. Consider playing a special song in the background.

VIDEO MONTAGE DURING
THE CEREMONY ****

At a recent ceremony held on a theater stage, the bride and groom took advantage of their unique setting by presenting a video montage during their ceremony. At the appointed time, a screen was lowered from above and the guests all got to enjoy a short slideshow of photos of the bride and groom growing up, enjoying memorable moments with their family and friends, and falling in love with each other. Your ceremony setting will determine whether or not this idea will be feasible.

FLOWER PETAL TOSS *

Provide paper cones filled with flower petals on the inside ends of each row of chairs or pews. Have your officiant instruct your guests to get them ready just before he introduces you as husband and wife and sends you down the aisle. While you are making your exit, they can shower you with flower petals.

BUTTERFLY RELEASE **

Provide each guest with a small paper box holding a monarch butterfly. Your officiant instructs the guests to get them ready just before he introduces you as husband and wife and sends you down the aisle. While you are making your exit, the butterflies will be released. Securing the butterflies and keeping them alive can be a little precarious, but the moment created when they are released can be quite striking.

DOVE RELEASE ***

You are presented with live doves to hold in your hands while the officiant shares how their release symbolizes your new beginning as husband and wife. The doves are released as your guests cheer.

BRING IN A BAGPIPER ★★★★

Nothing fills the air with a feeling of electricity quite like the sound of bagpipes. A bagpiper can turn your ceremony processional and/or recessional into a truly memorable moment. You won't need to worry about amplification, as bagpipes are loud enough on their own.

THE SABER ARCH FOR THE RECESSIONAL ★★★

At one wedding ceremony, the groom, an officer in the Marines Corps, asked a few of his friends to show up in their dress blues with their sabers. As the ceremony ended, they raised their sabers from either side of the aisle, forming a saber arch under which the bride and groom made their exit. As the bride and groom approached the last set of sabers, one of the Marines lowered his saber to block their progress until the groom gave the bride one more kiss. After they kissed and he let them pass, he gave the bride a swift swat on the rear end with his saber. Granted, the swat could be seen as an example of misogyny, but it has been part of the "traditional" way the Marines Corps has conducted a saber arch for many years.

THE RECEIVING LINE IN THE AISLE ★★

The receiving line is one way to make sure you get a chance to greet each of your guests. However, the most common complaint about receiving lines is that they can take too long and add more delays to the post-ceremony photos as well as the start time for the reception. With your best man, maid of honor, and parents greeting each guest before they get to greet the two of you, it's pretty obvious why the receiving line has a reputation for dragging on too long. But if you are committed to the idea of greeting each and every guest, here is another option that might save some time. After your wedding party members and parents have exited down the aisle, your officiant can announce that the two of you would like to greet and thank each guest for coming. At that point, the two of you can come back down the aisle and greet each row of guests as they stand and make their exit. The rest of guests will be more comfortable waiting in their seats and the guests who are leaving will be more inclined to keep their comments brief as they can see all of the remaining guests who are waiting for their turn.

MARK & MELISSA

AUGUST 5, 2005
RINGWOOD, NEW JERSEY

"Mazel Tov!"

With a last name like Pedalino, it's fairly obvious that Mark is Italian. However, as a popular bar/bat mitzvah entertainer, his respect for the Jewish traditions was evident during their wedding ceremony. Mark was escorted forward by his father and mother. Melissa was also escorted down the aisle by her mom and dad. Finally, before they were presented as husband and wife, Mark stepped down firmly on the glass to break it as their guests all shouted…"Mazel Tov!"

CEREMONY AGENDA

5:00–6:30
Drinks & Appetizers

6:30
Guests Begin Seating
"Bolero"
by Maurice Ravel

6:40
Ceremony Begins
Seating of Grandparents
"Canon In D Major"
by Johann Pachelbel

Groomsmen's Processional
* *"Crazy Little Thing Called Love"*
by Michael Bublé

Groom's Processional
* *"Crazy Little Thing Called Love"*
by Queen

Bridesmaid's Processional
"These Are Days"
by 10,000 Maniacs

Bride's Processional
"You Are So Beautiful"
by Joe Cocker

Ceremony
Officiated by:
Rev. Randy Bartlett

Nuptial Blessing
Read by:
Grandma Dora Pedalino

7:20
Recessional
"Then He Kissed Me"
by The Crystals
"Finally"
by Ce Ce Peniston

7:30
Off to the Reception

* "CRAZY LITTLE THING CALLED LOVE"

Being a highly skilled Wedding Entertainment Director himself, Mark selected "Crazy Little Thing Called Love" by Michael Bublé to play as his groomsmen entered, followed by Queen's version of the same song mixed in at the a capella break as Mark made his own entrance… and then the guests all cheered!

CHAPTER 14
THE COCKTAIL HOUR

*W*hile you are finishing formal photos after the ceremony, the guests will be patiently waiting for your arrival at the reception. This is usually called the cocktail hour because the bar is now open and refreshments are often being served. Here are some ideas to make this time even more enjoyable.

BACKGROUND MUSIC SETS THE MOOD **

The atmosphere created by appropriate background music will make your guests feel more comfortable. Keep in mind that your selections should create the kind of ambience that will match your personal style, while complementing any themes you may have chosen for your wedding reception. Music that is too loud or that could be described as obnoxious by most of your guests should be avoided.

One couple had a '40s theme for the bride's hair and gown, the bridesmaids' hair and dresses, and even the décor. Putting together a mix of classic vocal jazz artists like Frank Sinatra, Dean Martin, Ella Fitzgerald, Nat King Cole, and Billie Holiday, while featuring their best songs about love, was a perfect match.

Another bride and groom requested a fun mix of alternative listening hits from the 1980s. Songs like "Bette Davis Eyes" by Kim Carnes, "Down Under" by Men At Work, "Steppin' Out" by Joe Jackson, and "99 Red Balloons" by Nena filled the air. The guests started getting the idea that they would be in for a fun celebration in just a little while.

EVERYBODY LOVES A CHOCOLATE FOUNTAIN **

When the smell of melted chocolate begins to fill the air, your guests' mouths will begin to water. With sliced fruit, marshmallows, graham crackers, and Rice Krispie treats for dipping, your friends and family members will enjoy a light dessert while they await your arrival.

DISPOSABLE CAMERAS *

Give your guests some disposable cameras so they can take fun photos of their own. When the reception is over, you get to collect the cameras and have the films developed. Ask the MC to remind the guests to leave the spent cameras on their tables. (Be sure to get quality disposable cameras, as some of the cheaper, generic brands tend to turn out considerably fewer quality images.)

AUTOGRAPHS ON YOUR ENGAGEMENT PORTRAIT *

Set up your framed engagement portrait on an easel with a matte border and invite your guests to leave their autographs on it for a keepsake. This idea can be carried over to other items as well. One couple provided the guests with a special marker so they could autograph a surfboard. When my wife, Lisa, and I got married, a friend made up a large white vinyl banner with our names and wedding date printed on it. Our guests enjoyed signing their names all over it.

THE POLAROID/SCRAPBOOK GUEST BOOK **

Enlist the services of a friend or family member to take Polaroid pictures of each person, couple, or family in attendance, and then invite them to write a special message for the bride and groom on the scrapbook page adjacent to their photo. This can also be done with a digital camera with a compatible printer. You can also use this idea with stickers and markers to make a scrapbook.

INVITE YOUR GUESTS TO PAINT A MASTERPIECE **

At a recent Valentine's Day wedding, the guests were invited to pick up a brush and make their own mark on a blank canvas with several different colors of paint. The painting their guests created is now hanging in the couple's home as a reminder of the love their guests affirmed for them on their wedding day.

RENT A PHOTO BOOTH ***

Rent a photo booth for the day and invite your guests to sit inside and get their

pictures taken. They can then cut and paste their pictures into a scrapbook and write a personalized note to the bride and groom. I saw a photo booth keep the guests entertained for the entire evening at a reception. Even the bride and groom stepped inside to take some photos while feeding each other cake. More information on renting a photo booth can be found at these two Web sites, PhotoBoothScrapbooks.com and FotoCabina.com.

HAVE A CARICATURE ARTIST DRAW YOUR GUESTS ***

At one wedding, the guests were given the opportunity to sit for a caricature artist. The artist kept them entertained during the cocktail hour and beyond, and the guests took these unique keepsakes home with them.

WORDS OF WISDOM CARDS **

Provide note cards, pens, and a receptacle. Ask your guests to put their names on one side of the card and their best words of wisdom for a long and happy marriage on the other. The cards can be placed in a small box or treasure chest as a keepsake. They can also be used to fill a scrapbook.

"WHAT DOES LOVE MEAN TO YOU?" CARDS **

Along the same lines as the previous idea, Mitch Taylor, a Wedding Entertainment Director in Gladstone, Michigan, says, "Have your guests write their own answers to the question 'What Does Love Mean To You?' on 3x5 cards and then deposit them in special box so the two of you can read them later."

BRIDE & GROOM TRIVIA MIXER **

Make a list of things about the two of you, each of which is known by only one person among your group of guests. Print up the list with blanks for the answers to be filled in by your guests. Be sure your guests know that the answers are known only by one person per question. This will keep the participants busy as they will have to ask most, if not all, of your guests for the answers they are seeking. You might even offer a prize to the first person who can get all of the correct answers. Those that participate will not only learn more about the two of you in the process, but they will also get to know quite a few of your guests.

THE ARTSY SCAVENGER HUNT *

At a cocktail hour at a museum, Mike Anderson, a Wedding Entertainment Director in Sacramento, California, came up with this idea. "We gave the guests a checklist of various paintings and sculptures in the museum. While the bride and groom were finishing their photos, the guests made their way through the museum. Whoever was able to 'collect' the largest number of items on the list was rewarded with a Best Buy gift card."

THE PHOTO SCAVENGER HUNT *

Provide your guests with a list of unique "items" to capture in a photo on their digital cameras. The items could include a kiss, a bouquet, a snack, a drink, a gift, a shoe, the groom's wedding ring, the bride's dress, etc. This idea will not only keep your guests entertained, but it might also give you some really great photos that might not have been captured otherwise. You could offer a prize for the best photo or the largest collection of photos gathered.

DISPLAY A LOOPED VIDEO MONTAGE ★★★

Have someone create a short video montage about the two of you. Play it continually on a small television, monitor, or a laptop screen throughout your cocktail hour. If you already have background music playing, I recommend you mute the audio portion of the video montage.

BRING IN A MAGICIAN ★★★★

When one of your guests suddenly makes a coin disappear, the guests who are nearby will realize they're in for a treat. Magicians who specialize in close-up magic tricks can blend into your crowd putting on spontaneous, mini-performances for groups of five to ten at a time. Soon your crowd will be buzzing with conversation as your guests ask each other: "How did he do that?"

CREATIVE PHOTOS FOR TABLE NUMBERS ★★

Wedding Entertainment Director Jim Cerone, based in Indianapolis, says, "Create your own table numbers featuring photos of the two of you in a variety of fun and meaningful locations. Have a friend snap the photos during an afternoon road trip from one site to the next while you hold up a hand-painted sign with a different table number at each location. When your guests see these, they will soon begin making new friends as they wander the room to see the different photos that have been created for each table."

CHAPTER 15
THE GRAND ENTRANCE

*M*any entertainers believe that loud music and even louder introductions are the key ingredients for creating a memorable performance. It may be memorable, but maybe not for the right reasons. Your grand entrance will set the tone for the rest of your reception. If this moment is used to create connections that are informative, entertaining, personalized, and emotional, your guests will feel more involved and will have more fun. In this chapter, we will examine how you can make your introductions unique, humorous, creative, and even dramatic. Let's make it grand!

JUST THE TWO OF US **

The simplest grand entrance involves just introducing the two of you into the reception while your guests are encouraged to stand and cheer. This is a moment your guests have been waiting for and they will greet you both with smiles and applause.

MEET THE PARENTS ***

Taking a moment to properly introduce your parents provides an opportunity to show them some much deserved gratitude. You can simply ask them to stand at their tables as the guests applaud, or they can be invited to enter the room as they are announced, preceding the wedding party's introductions. If any of your parents have been divorced or are remarried, be sure to clarify with your MC how and in what order you would like them to be introduced.

THE LITTLE ANGELS ***

If you have a flower girl(s) and/or a ring bearer(s), and they are ready for a moment in the spotlight, feel free to have them introduced as well. You might need someone in the room to collect them so they don't get overwhelmed and become unsure about where to go.

IT'S RAINING MEN! ✳✳✳

If you have ushers who are not part of your wedding party, feel free to have them introduced before bringing in your wedding party.

HERE COMES THE WEDDING PARTY ✳✳✳

There is no "right" or "standard" formula for bringing in your wedding party, but it's always lots of fun. Working through the lineup, you can have them introduced as couples and end with your best man and maid/matron of honor. They can be introduced one person at a time, alternating the bridesmaids with the groomsmen, or the bridesmaids one at a time, followed by the groomsmen one at a time. You could have them come in all at once as one big group.

LADIES FIRST...MEN SECOND ✳✳✳✳

At one reception, the bride and groom wanted to watch their wedding party members be introduced, but they also wanted to enter the room last. To accommodate their wishes, we introduced all of the bridesmaids first as a group. When they arrived at the staging point in front of the dance floor, each bridesmaid was invited to step forward as we delivered a personalized introduction with some humorous sound bites. We brought in the groomsmen next and introduced them the same way. The guests were too busy watching the bridesmaids and groomsmen to notice that the bride and groom were watching the whole thing from the doorway.

INTRODUCE THE BRIDE AND GROOM FIRST
*****

Andy Austin, a popular wedding entertainer from Dallas, says, "Tradition dictates the bride and groom, as the guests of honor, are to be introduced last, following the parents and the wedding party. But if you are planning on introducing your wedding party members with personalized theme songs or humorous biographical introductions, then why not turn tradition on its head and have your MC introduce the two of you first. This will allow you to enjoy the fun created by the wedding party's introductions along with your guests instead of trying to see what's happening from the outside. It will also give your wedding party members a familiar destination, as they'll be instructed to go stand with you or go greet you with a hug when they enter the reception."

WHO'S GETTING INTRODUCED NEXT? *****

At a recent reception, the bride and groom opted to be introduced first and then we invited the wedding party to crowd into the wide doorway as one big group. The wedding party members had no idea of the order in which they would be introduced. They were instructed to listen to the biographical introductions the bride and groom had written for them and when they recognized that they were the one being introduced, they were to take two steps forward. The guests enjoyed watching them try to figure out who was next, and the laughter was only enhanced by seeing the whole group laughing instead of just the person being introduced. Their individual introductions were concluded when we finally said their name (". . . she's our matron of honor, Ashley Hart!"). Then, as the crowd began to cheer, we played a personalized theme song for each person as he or she went over to greet the bride and groom with a hug.

THANK AND WELCOME YOUR GUESTS ****

Wedding Entertainment Director Randy Bartlett of Sacramento, California, says, "Immediately following your grand entrance, while all of your guests are still standing and cheering your arrival, take advantage of the moment to express your gratitude to your guests for coming to help you celebrate. You can use this opportunity to thank your parents for their support. The groom could also acknowledge his thoughts and feelings about his bride. Be sure to tell your MC in advance that you want to do this and ask for a cordless handheld microphone so you can thank and welcome your guests from the center of the room following your entrance. Your band or DJ should also be instructed in advance to kill the music as soon as you start speaking."

CREATE SOME ENERGY WITH THEME MUSIC ***

Rather than just making these introductions as announcements, make this a production by adding theme music. You can choose a dramatic theme song that will start playing just as the two of you enter the room. You can select a separate theme song to play as your wedding party is being introduced. You can even pick out theme songs for your parents, the ushers, and the ring bearer and flower girl.

This can be personalized further by choosing a different song for each couple in your wedding party, or a theme song for each person — maybe even a song that really sums up their personality or what they do for a living. You'll need to discuss your theme song ideas with your entertainment vendor to make sure he owns, or can play, the songs you want. Also, you may want to clearly communicate where you want the songs to begin. I once watched a DJ on video introduce the bride's parents to the song "Jesse's Girl" by Rick Springfield, as her father was named Jesse. But the song starts off soft and it was faded out well before it got to the title portion of the chorus. Most of the guests missed the homage to the bride's father's name because the DJ started the song from the beginning rather than selecting a cue point that would have been more meaningful.

ERIK & AARICA

NOVEMBER 7, 2008
PHOENIX, ARIZONA

Sleeves . . . Who Needs 'Em?

As Erik and Aarica were brought into their reception with a love story introduction, Erik had his jacket slung over his shoulder. Upon sharing that at their first meeting Erik had been wearing his typical sleeveless shirt, his friends and family began to laugh in agreement. But they began to howl even louder when Aarica suddenly reached over and ripped his tux shirtsleeves right off his arms.

* BIRTHDAY SPOTLIGHT

Erik and Aarica decided to share the first pieces of their cake with three of their guests who were celebrating birthdays. They put lit candles on their slices of cake and invited the rest of the guests to serenade them with "Happy Birthday."

RECEPTION AGENDA

5:30–6:30
Drinks & Appetizers

6:35
Grand Entrance
"Rocket"
by Def Leppard

6:45–7:45
Dinner

7:45
Cake Cutting
"Grow Old With You"
by Adam Sandler

"Knock Me A Kiss"
by Louis Jordan

7:55
* Birthday Spotlight

8:00
Toasts
"Birthday"
by The Beatles

8:30–8:45
The Special Dances
First Dance
"All My Life"
by K-Ci & JoJo

Father/Daughter Dance
"Because You Loved Me"
by Celine Dion

Mother/Son Dance
"Unforgettable"
by Natalie & Nat King Cole

8:45–9:20
Open Dancing

9:20
Bouquet & Garter Toss
"I Got It From My Mama"
by Will.I.Am

"Pour Some Sugar On Me"
by Def Leppard

"NFL Theme"
by Scott Schreer

9:30–11:00
Open Dancing

11:00
Last Dance
"Con Te Partirò"
by Andrea Bocelli

TURN ON THE SPOTLIGHT
*****

Lighting effects can dramatically enhance a well-produced grand entrance. When the house lights go down and several spotlights begin spinning around the room in tempo to the music, your guests will begin to cheer before you even get in the room. Spotlights can be used to highlight the doorway where your wedding party will be entering. The spotlights can then follow you as you enter the room. It is very important to make sure that your entertainment vendor has the right technology and expertise to produce these lighting effects properly.

THE SABER ARCH ENTRANCE ***

Some military weddings may choose to utilize the saber arch as part of the grand entrance. The uniformed saber guard can stand on either side of the entry as the wedding party members come through. Then, when the bride and groom are introduced, the saber guard will raise their sabers to form an arch for the bride and groom to enter under and through. A sports theme could be incorporated using baseball bats, hockey sticks, or even paintball guns to form the arch. A Star Wars theme could be created using lighted toy light sabers. You could even have your bridesmaids and groomsmen line up on either side of the entry point and form an arch with their outstretched arms.

THE TUNNEL OF LOVE ENTRANCE *****

Build on the saber arch idea with a romantic twist, suggests Larry Williams, a Wedding Entertainment Director based in Reno. "The wedding party members are instructed to line up across from each other, creating a pathway extending from the reception's entry point. They are each given a long stemmed rose in advance, and after all of the adult wedding party members have been introduced, they hold their roses out high, creating an arch for the bride and groom's entrance. Then the flower girl is introduced and she drops rose petals on the pathway as she enters. Finally, the bride and groom are introduced. 'All You Need Is Love' by the Beatles is one example of a great song to play, because it begins with a trumpet fanfare followed by the lyrics 'Love, Love, Love...' The wedding party can than present their roses to the bride and groom, or to any of the bride and groom's immediate family members, or they can just throw them in the air above the bride and groom to shower them with roses."

THE AWESOME BLOSSOM ENTRANCE ****

Sacramento-based Wedding Entertainment Director Mike Anderson suggests, "Have your wedding party come back to the entry point after they have all been introduced. Having rehearsed their part in advance, the bridesmaids and groomsmen form a circle with their arms pointing into the center of the circle. With their wedding party's bodies blocking the entry point, the bride and groom sneak unseen into the center of the circle as the bridesmaids and groomsmen raise and lower their arms and shoulders like a rolling wave. On cue, with a loud shout, the circled group will throw their hands straight up and out as they lower themselves to their knees, revealing the bride and groom standing in the center of a blossoming human flower."

ATTACK OF THE PAPARAZZI! ****

This creative idea has been suggested by Scott Faver, a nationally known DJ trainer and wedding entertainer from Phoenix. "Have your MC instruct the guests to grab their cameras and/or any disposable cameras that have been provided and get ready to give the two of you a special welcome upon your introduction. As soon as you walk through the doors, you will be mobbed as dozens of your guests armed with cameras suddenly begin swarming around you snapping pictures as if the two of you are Hollywood's latest power couple and they are the paparazzi!"

THE HAND-DRAWN CARRIAGE ENTRANCE ****

Kevin Cordova, a popular wedding entertainer in Las Vegas, suggests, "On her wedding day, every bride wants to be treated like a princess. This can be clearly seen when the bride arrives for her ceremony on a white, horse-drawn carriage. Since most receptions take place indoors, a horse-drawn carriage would rarely

be possible for a grand entrance into the celebration. However, I was able find an elegant, white, hand-drawn carriage that could be pulled into the room by two ushers or two groomsmen. The carriage can be drawn to the center of the dance floor with the bride and groom riding inside and giving their best parade waves to their guests."

THE SHADOW ENTRANCE *****

Another creative entrance suggested by Mike Anderson of Creative Memories Entertainment in Sacramento is the shadow entrance. "I was inspired by the shadow show that was demonstrated by Prince during the 2007 Super Bowl halftime show. Using a billowing white sheet with light projected from behind, Prince appeared as a 40-foot shadow image during his guitar solo. When one of my couples selected a reception location that featured a stage with a rear projected screen, I suggested to them that we might want to create a unique grand entrance using their shadows on that screen. I introduced the wedding party members into the room and they began to line up on the stage on either side of the screen, which at the time was only displaying a color monogram of the bride and groom's initials. When it was time to introduce the bride and groom, a white light suddenly shown from behind the screen, illuminating 20-foot-tall shadows of the bride and dancing with their hands in the air. As the music continued to build in energy, I introduced them as the screen began to rise and they walked forward to join the rest of their wedding party on the stage with the white light shining brightly behind them. The guests leapt to their feet and began cheering as loudly as I've ever heard at a wedding." (You can see a video of this effect in action on Mike's Web site, http://www.CreativeMemoriesDJ. com/tbwreshadow.html).

THE REVERSE GRAND ENTRANCE ****

Here is another example of a creative entrance submitted by Bill Hermann, a Wedding Entertainment Director based in Minneapolis. "The father of the bride decided to host his daughter's reception in his private airplane hangar. Because they had put a considerable amount of time and money designing and decorating the hangar to create a setting that was quite extraordinary, we decided to take a lesson from Extreme Home Makeover and do a 'reveal' to the guests. As the bride, groom, and their families waited inside, the main hangar doors were opened to reveal their amazing reception décor. Over 300 guests were awestruck and cheered as they entered the beautifully decorated hangar."

INCORPORATE A STYLISTIC THEME ****

How about creating a grand entrance that resembles other well-produced introductions? Sporting events, movies, or game shows can all be sources of inspiration. For instance, using a basketball theme, introduce your bridesmaids and groomsmen like this: "Standing a full 6-foot-1 and hailing from Bergen Community College…show some love for our best man . . . Dave Miller!" You could even use their college fight songs for theme music.

Using a movie theme, your bridesmaids and groomsmen could be introduced into the room wearing outfits from the '60s while songs from the Austin Powers or the Grease soundtracks are played. Using a game show theme, your bridesmaids and groomsmen could be introduced as contestants on *The Dating Game*: "An accountant by day and a party girl by night . . . she's a Cancer who enjoys watching reruns of *Will & Grace* and taking long, moonlit walks on the beach with strange men. Let's hear it for the maid of honor . . . Lisa Forrette!" Of course, the "Dating Game theme music" would be playing.

You could play the theme music from *Masterpiece Theater* just before the two of you make your entrance, and have your MC give your guests a look back into the historical moments that occurred on your wedding date. "On this day in history, in 1796, America welcomed its very first elephant. In 1899, the inventor of Scrabble was born. His name was Alfred Butts. And in 1967, The Turtles were at number 1 on the pop charts…with 'Happy Together.' But these moments all pale in comparison to the one you have all witnessed today! And now, here they are for the very first time in recorded history … The new Mr. And Mrs. Jeremy Brown!''

Your MC will absolutely need to know how to write humor, while also demonstrating that he is highly skilled in the art of being funny without coming off as cheesy, canned, or inappropriate.

THE ITALIAN GRAND ENTRANCE ****

Bill Hermann also shares this suggestion: "For an Italian groom who wanted to add a slight Italian flavor to his reception, and building on his love for the music of Dean Martin, we introduced the bride and groom into the room to the tune of 'Ain't That A Kick In The Head' by Dean Martin. Once they were in the center of the room, the music was faded down quickly and the guests all began waving white napkins while singing 'That's Amoré' with lyric sheets that I had provided in advance."

THE NASCAR GRAND ENTRANCE ****

Ron Ruth, a Wedding Entertainment Director based in Kansas City, Missouri, shares, "I had a bride and groom who were really into NASCAR. Instead of simply introducing them into the room, I provided the wedding party with checkered

flags and had them line up at the doorway with the bridesmaids on one side and the groomsmen on the other. There were also four checkered flags on each table throughout the ballroom. As I led up to the actual introduction of the bride and groom, I included the sound effect of a NASCAR engine revving up with the NASCAR theme song building in the background. The actual wording included: 'Ladies and gentlemen … start your engines … and celebrate the winning lap with your guests of honor . . . Mr. And Mrs . . . 'The wedding party then waved their checkered flags as the bride and groom entered the room. The guests followed suit and waved their checkered flags while cheering."

THE BASEBALL GRAND ENTRANCE ★★★★

Here is another suggestion from Ron Ruth: "The bride and groom were huge baseball fans. The groom actually proposed to the bride on the pitcher's mound of the Little League field where he had played as a child. Not only did the bride say 'yes,' she also ran the bases afterwards as if she had hit a home run. How do you not include that story into the introduction? I was able to purchase several dozen hollow plastic balls that looked incredibly like real baseballs and I had the couple autograph them, including the date of their wedding, in advance of their reception. I filled two pails with autographed balls, and placed them on the dance floor prior to the introduction. As I told the story of their proposal, the guests could hear the sound effect of the crack of a bat and a stadium full of fans cheering followed by an edited version of 'Centerfield' by John Fogerty, which began just as I introduced the couple by name. When the bride and groom reached the dance floor, the music continued to play as they each picked up a pail of balls and went around the room tossing them out to their guests. Their guests loved it and began clamoring to get a ball of their own."

THE MAIN STREET ELECTRICAL PARADE ENTRANCE ★★★★★

Mike Anderson created another entrance: "I had a couple who had first met while working together at Disneyland. I suggested that we could use the 'Main Street Electrical Parade' theme music for their grand entrance. They loved the idea. To add even more of an impact, I suggested we get glow necklaces for all of the guests to wave in the air. I dimmed the lights and spotlighted the wedding party as they entered the room. Each member of the wedding party had flashing lights and we decorated the bride's bouquet with LED lights to add to the overall effect."

One of my couples wanted to build on that idea. At their request, I created a special version of the 'Main Street Electrical Parade' theme music for them. We edited out the Disneyland "electrified" voice message in the beginning of the song and replaced it with my own voice-over message introducing the bride and groom in the same singsong effect as the original. Then we arranged for the bride and groom to enter their reception (with all the lights turned off and the guests standing, cheering, and waving the glow necklaces over their heads), covered in battery-powered, white Christmas twinkle lights and spinning as if they were floats in the famous Disneyland parade. It was one of the most amazing entrances I have ever witnessed.

SHOW OFF SOME HIDDEN TALENTS *****

If one or more of your wedding party members has a unique ability or specialized skill that could be entertaining, find a way for your MC to coax them into showcasing their hidden talents during the introductions. At one of my receptions, a groomsman named Micah was known for his unique dance referred to as "The Micah Man Dance." I found out that he would only do this dance to an '80s rap song called "Take It To Da House" by Trick Daddy. At the right moment, the guests were told about his special dance and the music was started. Everyone began to cheer and sure enough, he did "The Micah Man Dance"!

At another reception, one of the groomsmen was an actor skilled in imitating regional dialects. I gave him a cordless microphone and, with no advance warning, told him to share his thoughts on the ceremony in the voice of an Italian from Long Island. Without a moment's hesitation, he began to riff about the ceremony in the requested dialect and all of the guests burst into laughter. Perhaps one of your wedding party members likes to sing karaoke to one particular song, or is a wealth of sports trivia going back decades, or can quote obscure lines from popular movies. Any of these ideas and more can be turned into a quick entertaining moment.

START YOUR OWN DANCE CONTEST ***

Here's another idea from wedding entertainer Andy Austin. "Challenge your wedding party members to try and top each other with some funny dance moves as they enter the room and step onto the dance floor. If the ushers will be entering first, get them to set the bar high by tearing off their jackets and swinging them over their heads. Each couple that follows will have to come up with their own routines and your guests will be roaring with laughter and applause."

DANCE WITH THE ONE WHO BROUGHT YOU ***

At one energetic reception, the bride and groom opted to have their wedding party members be introduced with their dates or spouses instead of the bridesmaid or groomsman they had walked with in the ceremony. Borrowing from the dance contest idea, they challenged each couple to put on their best moves as they crossed the dance floor. To help them with this effort, the bride and groom selected a different high energy dance song for each couple. One of the groomsmen decided to raise the bar (and the energy level in the room) by dropping to the dance floor to do "the worm."

PERSONALIZED BIOGRAPHICAL INTRODUCTIONS *****

Write a short biographical introduction for your MC to deliver about each wedding party member as they enter. You can include information about your relationship (relative/friend/how long), where they live, their occupation and/or educational status (i.e., college student, high school student), their relationship status (single/engaged/married), their hobbies, reasons why they might be "famous," what their friends would vote them most likely to do in life, an embarrassing story, or what their friendship means to you on a personal level. The size of your wedding party should determine how much detail can go into each scripted bio. If you have a large wedding party, keep it short so your grand entrance won't feel too long.

INTRODUCE YOUR OWN WEDDING PARTY MEMBERS ****

If you decide to create personalized bios, another option would be for the two of you to deliver these introductions yourselves. You will need a cordless microphone if you intend to read the script from outside the room. One couple took this idea to a new level. The groom worked in video production, so they created their own prerecorded, personalized, biographical introductions on a DVD featuring photomontages of them with each wedding party member. The wedding party members were able to watch their individual videos along with the guests.

INCORPORATE HUMOROUS SOUND CLIPS *****

Add fun sound clips to enhance your personalized biographical introductions. These can include movie clips, sound effects, song clips, and special recordings. Movie clips can be used to gently poke fun at your wedding party. When introducing the bride's only brother, you could say that his first reaction to the news of their engagement sounded like this… (and then play a clip from *Tommy Boy* where Chris Farley's character says, "Brother?…I'm gonna have a brother? I've always dreamed about having a brother!").

Sound effects can be used as a punch line for a joke about the small town where one groomsman lives. When you play sound effects of crickets chirping and cows mooing, the guests will enjoy a good laugh. Song clips can be used to highlight a groomsman's occupation. If he is a stock broker, the theme song from *The Apprentice*, with the lyrics "Money, Money, Money," will get a good reaction. And finally, special recordings can really create memorable moments. At one reception, one of the bridesmaids was a reporter for her local television station. Thanks to the Internet, we were able to record a short clip from one of her stories with the lead anchorman thanking her by name as she finished. She was completely surprised to hear her own voice and her reaction resulted in a great swell of laughter from the crowd. The timing issues are critical for pulling this off in a manner that will let your guests know that they are about to experience "The Best Wedding Reception…Ever!"

RYAN & CELENA

AUGUST 30, 2008
LAGUNA BEACH, CALIFORNIA

Happy Birthday to the Maid of Honor

Celena's sister, Courtney, was celebrating her birthday on the day of their wedding. Ryan and Celena decided to surprise her by having their guests sing "Happy Birthday" to her just before she was about give her Maid of Honor's toast. Courtney was pleasantly surprised and she was still able to pull off a very thoughtful toast.

* GRAND ENTRANCE

Ryan and Celena wanted their reception to be filled with high-energy dance music. They selected a different energetic entrance song for each member of their wedding party and invited them to enter with their date or spouse. Each couple was challenged to put on their best moves as they crossed the dance floor with the guests cheering.

RECEPTION AGENDA

6:30–7:45
Drinks & Appetizers

7:45
* Grand Entrance
"Sweet Dreams (Are Made Of This)
[Hot Remix]"
by Eurythmics

7:55
First Dance
"When I'm With You"
by Sheriff

8:00
Fathers' Toasts

8:10–9:10
Dinner

8:25
Father/Daughter Dance
"Have I Told You Lately"
by Rod Stewart

8:30
Mother/Son Dance
"I Hope You Dance"
by Lee Ann Womack

9:10
Formal Toasts

9:20–9:45
Open Dancing

9:45
Cake Cutting
"Pour Some Sugar On Me"
by Def Leppard
"Knock Me A Kiss"
by Louis Jordan

10:00
Money Dance

10:15
Bouquet Toss
"Express Yourself"
by Madonna

10:20–12:00 a.m.
Open Dancing

12:00 a.m.
Last Dance
"At Last"
by Etta James

CHAPTER 16
THE TOASTS

. . . .

*T*he formal toasts at your reception give the people closest to you a chance to share some sentimental anecdotes, words of appreciation, and best wishes for your future. Some who have been asked to make a formal toast will spend countless hours writing, rewriting, and rehearsing their presentation to make sure it properly conveys their truest thoughts and feelings. Others may wait until the moment they're introduced and then speak from the heart. Sadly, the latter example can often result in toasts featuring some unexpected and even off-color comments.

When it comes to preparing for a toast, Tom Haibeck, the author of Wedding Toasts Made Easy and The Wedding MC, says, "Far too many people just assume they can stand up before several hundred people and 'wing it' with a wedding toast. And that's THE most common reason why wedding toasts go awry — the people delivering them simply aren't prepared. As a result, they often get nervous and flustered, become incoherent, drone on way too long, venture into areas that are completely inappropriate, and embarrass themselves and others in the process."

Let's explore some creative ideas for making the formal toasts at your reception more polished, more memorable, and more uniquely personalized.

. . . .

PICK PEOPLE TO TOAST WHO ARE READY, WILLING, AND ABLE **

Your list should start with those who may already be expecting to make a toast, such as the best man, the maid/matron of honor, the bride's parents, the groom's parents, or even both of you — the bride and groom. Next, determine who really wants to give a toast, and who you really want (or don't want) to give a toast. Whomever you select to give a formal toast should be given plenty of advance notice so they can prepare. Consider buying them a book on preparing wedding

toasts as a thoughtful gift. Finally, don't be afraid to give them some guidelines regarding your thoughts on inappropriate content, time constraints, etc.

INVITE SOMEONE SPECIAL TO GIVE A BLESSING FOR THE MEAL *

Perhaps you'd like to include a relative or close friend in your festivities by asking them to say a blessing for the meal. If your wedding officiant is a friend of the family, he or she might be a good choice as well.

CREATE THE TOASTING ORDER BASED ON CONTENT *****

Wedding Entertainment Director Randy Bartlett says, "The formal toasts will usually vary in content and delivery. By discussing what will be said in advance with each person toasting, not only can I assist them in possibly delivering their toasts better, but I can also arrange the toasting order to build towards a big punch line that will get everyone laughing. Or we might start with a good laugh while leading to an emotionally poignant closing toast. The temperament of the bride and groom along with their guests will dictate for me which toasting order will be most effective at each reception." Someone else will need to create this lineup order, because you really shouldn't be privy to the contents of the formal toasts before they are delivered. Your MC is the most obvious person to entrust this to, but it is absolutely vital that you're sure the MC fully understands how to do this properly and effectively.

THE SHY GUY TOAST ✳✳✳

Jim Cerone, a Wedding Entertainment Director based in Indianapolis, shares the following example for helping a shy person feel more comfortable giving a formal toast. "The best man, and brother of the groom, was extremely nervous about giving his speech. While discussing this with him, all of the other groomsmen offered to help. I prepped them in advance and had them start at the far end of the head table, each giving a short comment before handing the microphone down the line. By the time it reached the best man, the crowd was already loosened up and laughing and he was much more relaxed and able to deliver a great toast."

MULTIMEDIA TOASTS ✳✳✳✳✳

If one or more of your toasters would like to use an audio sound clip, such as a special recorded message, or a song or movie clip, put them in touch with your entertainment vendor to discuss their needs and the timing for playing the clip in conjunction with their toasts. The same advice holds true if they want to show a short video as part of their toast. I once had a best man who brought in a projector with a screen at the last minute because he wanted to surprise the bride and groom with a video segment during his toast. This was also a big surprise to me. As the MC, I had to help him set up and test the equipment and run the audio through my sound system. Fortunately, because I found out about his surprise before the cocktail hour, I was able to assist him before the main reception was underway.

THE KEY TRICK ✳✳✳✳

A fun practical joke is to give a key to several of the ladies throughout the room, and then during the toasts, someone suggests that if anyone has an old house key for the groom's place, they should turn them in right away as he is now officially "off the market." If the groom is kept unaware that this will occur, he will begin turning several shades of red as more and more of the female guests start streaming up and dropping their keys on the head table. A good theme song could be "Just A Gigolo/I

Ain't Got Nobody" by David Lee Roth. You could even give a key or two to a few men for even more laughs. This idea is best when presented by your best man or your maid/matron of honor. Be sure your MC knows this will be happening as well and is ready with any special music cues.

GIVE A WELCOMING MESSAGE OF THANKS ✳✳✳

Take a moment when you first enter your reception, just after the formal toasts, or right after your cake cutting, to give a welcoming message thanking your guests for being an important part of your celebration and encouraging them to have a fun time. Be sure your MC knows you will be doing this and when, so he can make sure you have a microphone.

PRERECORDED TOASTS ✳✳✳

At a reception in October 2001, the groom's best friend (and also his first choice for best man) was unable to attend from the East Coast due to the tragic events of 9/11. The bride was able to secure a prerecorded toast from this valued friend. When it was played during the reception, it brought tears to the groom's eyes. If you have loved ones who won't be able to attend your reception, this can be a powerful way to include them in your celebration. Be sure your MC knows you will be doing this and when you'd like to do it.

"SURPRISE" TOASTS ✳✳✳✳

Do you have one or more friends who are gifted speakers and/or are naturally funny, but they have not been included in your celebration yet? Perhaps you would enjoy putting them on the spot? The "surprise" toasts can create some fun energy during the meal. The MC will have been given the names and seating locations of your victim(s). After the formal toasts have finished, the guests will be informed that there are still a few more toasts coming during the meal, but who will be giving them has not yet been determined. Then, when the guests least expect it, the MC will gather their attention while introducing the first person selected to give a "surprise" toast who, although completely unprepared, will be handed a cordless microphone as the MC walks away. If you choose your victim(s) wisely, this can create some very humorous memories.

BEST MAN WARRANTY PRANK ****

James Loram, a wedding entertainer based in Fullerton, California, suggests, "If your best man is known for pulling pranks and you'd like to pull one on him for once, get together in advance with the DJ, band, or MC to prepare this idea. When the best man is introduced for his toast and given a cordless handheld microphone by the MC, his mic will suddenly go dead. When the MC walks back over to check the mic, it will suddenly be working just fine. But when it is handed back to the best man, it will again appear to malfunction. The MC can then explain to everyone that the problem appears to be…a defective best man. The MC asks the groom if he brought his Best Man Warranty, and when the groom pulls the large folded letter marked WARRANTY from his inside jacket pocket, the best man will realize that he's been set up. The MC reads aloud the warranty letter, which will certainly be filled with several jokes at the best man's expense. When the reading is completed, the best man will be handed a now fully functional mic and chances are pretty good he'll be fairly speechless for a few moments."

OPEN INVITE FOR GUESTS TO TOAST ***

If you have the time and want to give your guests a chance to get in on the toasts, have your MC offer an opportunity for anyone else who might be interested to come up to the microphone and make a toast. The MC will need to be told in advance that this will be done and how long you would prefer the open toasting to last. This idea is not advisable for toasts that precede a finely timed meal service, as they could easily run longer than expected.

BRIAN & JENNIFER

MAY 6, 2006
SILVERADO CANYON, CALIFORNIA

The Formal Toasts on Instant Replay

The formal toasts presented by Jennifer's parents, along with both best men, and the matron and maid of honor were very well done. With some quick editing, a few of the most poignant and humorous comments (which had been recorded) were "mixed" into the song "Wonderful Tonight," which had been Brian and Jennifer's selection for their last dance. Everyone was amazed to hear the toasts replayed, creating an unforgettable moment.

* VIDEO MONTAGE

Just days before their wedding, Brian and Jennifer found themselves in a minor crisis. Apparently, the wrong songs had been used in their video montage DVD. With a little rehearsal, to get the timing down, we were able to mix the correct songs live on the spot. The guests never even knew.

RECEPTION AGENDA

6:00
Grand Entrance
"Beautiful Day" by U2

6:15–7:20
Toasts & Dinner

7:25–7:40
The Special Dances
First Dance
"After All"
by Cher & Peter Cetera
Father/Daughter Dance
"Butterfly Kisses"
by Bob Carlisle
Mother/Son Dance
"The Way You Look Tonight"
by Frank Sinatra
Wedding Party Dance
"We Are Family"
by Sister Sledge

7:40–8:05
Open Dancing

8:05
Longevity Dance
"Let's Stay Together"
by Al Green

8:10
Cake Cutting
"Sugar, Sugar"
by The Archies
"This Magic Moment"
by The Drifters

8:20
*Video Montage

8:35
Bouquet & Garter Toss
"Independent Woman"
by Destiny's Child
"Lady Marmalade"
from Moulin Rouge Sdtk
"I Melt With You"
by Modern English
"Start Me Up"
by The Rolling Stones

8:45–9:55
Open Dancing

9:55
Last Dance
"Wonderful Tonight" by Eric Clapton

THE MUSIC VIDEO TOAST ★★★★★

One of the most creative ideas I've seen implemented was the music video Matt McKnight produced for his best man's toast. He wrote and performed a parody of the music video "I'm On A Boat" by The Lonely Island. The original music video was showcased on Saturday Night Live and featured Andy Samberg and T-Pain rapping about being on a boat while cruising around on the deck of a luxury yacht. Matt wrote his own lyrics that told a story about the bride and groom's dating relationship, poked fun at the groom for being a "straight-up nerd" when he was a little kid, and reminding them not to drink too much because they still had the honeymoon. He filmed the video while riding on the front of a boat in several different settings and the chorus resounded each time with the lyrics "How 'Bout A Toast!" This idea took an enormous amount of effort, talent, and preparation to create and present. Luckily for us, the complete music video was posted on YouTube. You can view it for yourself here: http://www.youtube.com/watch?v=cQkNWBYYnKc.

CHAPTER 17
THE MEAL

*T*he meal is often overlooked as a time for allowing your guests to feel more involved in your reception. Often the entertainment vendors take a break and throw on the same old background music they play at every wedding because, after all, people are eating so the fun can't begin until their plates have been cleared, right? WRONG! Depending on how many courses are served and your total guest count, the meal could last anywhere from just 45 minutes to well over two hours! That's a long time for your guests to be left wondering when the fun and dancing will get started. Don't forget, a reception is supposed to be a celebration, not just a fancy dinner. In this chapter, we will uncover methods for adding life to the meal while also encouraging your guests to become active participants, so they won't be left feeling like spectators.

BACKGROUND MUSIC CAN BUILD ENERGY **

As mentioned above, at many wedding receptions the background music played during the meal might be best described as the "default setting." Whether you have chosen to go with a band or hire a DJ, the background music choices played during the meal should be yours and yours alone. Keep in mind that your selections should start to build some energy in a manner that will match your personal style, while complementing any themes you may have chosen for your wedding reception. Music that is too loud or would best be described as obnoxious by most of your guests should be avoided in favor of music that is lighthearted and unobtrusive.

At a Malibu reception a few years ago, the bride and groom's list of background music included mildly upbeat selections from artists like Jack Johnson, John Mayer, Dave Matthews Band, Coldplay, Ben Harper, Euge Groove, Norah Jones, David Grey, and Keane. As the meal ended, the guests were having fun and they were ready to start dancing.

THE KISSING COUPLES DRAWING ****

It's fairly common at wedding receptions for the guests to clink on their glasses as a signal that they want the bride and groom to kiss. Build on this tradition by adding a fun twist. Provide your MC with a list of several other couples (married, engaged, and dating) who will be in attendance. Then have the MC instruct your guests that each time they tap on their drinking glasses and the two of you kiss, another couple will be randomly selected from the list and called upon to stand and kiss while your guests cheer them on. If you are both more outgoing and slightly daring, you could require that the randomly selected couple kiss first, and then the two of you must imitate their unique kiss. Soon your guests will be finding fun and creative ways to make the two of you kiss.

KISSING COUPLES WITH A CATCH PHRASE TWIST *****

A few years ago, I had the pleasure of watching Minneapolis-based Wedding Entertainment Director Bill Hermann turn a bride and groom's passion for word games into a kissing activity. "My couple wanted to find a way to get some of their guests to play Catch Phrase at their reception. They gave me a list of couples who they thought might make good 'contestants.' Then they created several large posters with a single word or phrase printed on them in a large font size. We told the guests that whenever they began tapping their glasses to make the bride and groom kiss, we would instead start a new Catch Phrase contest. One couple would be randomly selected from the list and called up to the front of the head table. The selected couple would be asked to choose which one of them would give clues and which one would try to guess the answer. The person trying to guess would be asked to turn his back to the head table and then the bride and groom would raise a randomly selected poster so the guests could see the word or phrase (except the person guessing, of course). The person giving the clues cannot use the actual word or phrase or any words or phrases that rhyme with it. If the person guessing is able to correctly identify the word or phrase within 30 seconds, the bride and groom will reward them by giving each other a kiss. But if the couple fails to correctly guess the word or phrase, then they will be asked to give each other a kiss or do some other random activity as their penalty."

PROGRESSIVE PASSION KISSING ***

Bill Hermann suggests another fun kissing activity. "Each time the glasses get tapped

by the guests, it is up to the bride and the groom to do 'one better' than their previous kiss. The couple must be ready to do more than a few kisses. The MC should go over this activity with the bride and groom in advance and offer advice on how to start off slow, getting more creative as the evening goes on, saving their best 'climactic' kiss for the finale."

SINGING TABLES FOR KISSES ★★★★

Ben Miller, a Wedding Entertainment Director from Illinois, says, "Try telling your guests that tapping on their drinking glasses to make you kiss just won't work at your reception. Have your MC inform them that as an alternative, if they stand as a table and sing any portion of a song that includes the word 'Love,' then and only then, will you kiss for them. If your group is already going to be just a little rowdy, soon you may have tables competing to see who can come up with the most creative song." I once heard the theme song for Oscar Mayer bologna during a reception. That's right, the word "love" is in there. This activity is not advisable with a buffet or food station meal, because many guests may not be seated at the same time. Also, it should be noted that a band may not be able to stop playing when the guests start singing as easily as a DJ can fade down any background music.

APPOINT "KISSING JUDGES" *****

This humorous option can be combined with any of the kissing contests. Jim and Denise Sanchez, a wedding entertainment team from Southern California, suggest: "Have your MC provide one select table of guests (perhaps the group that is clearly going to be the 'rowdy table') to serve as 'Kissing Judges.' The MC will provide them with large scorecards numbered 1-5, just like those used by the judges at ice skating competitions. When the bride and groom kiss, the 'Kissing Judges' will raise the scorecards and deliver their verdict. If your overall scores are too low, the bride and groom (and/or any additional couples) will be told to try again to see if they can get a better overall score. Soon, your guests will be trying to make you kiss again, just to see how well the judges will score you. There will undoubtedly be lots of laughter as your guests will cheer you on to a perfect score."

LET THE KISSING GAMES BEGIN! ****

Jay Sims, a Chicago-based Wedding Entertainment Director, suggests, "Consider making one of your favorite sports or competitive activities into a unique kissing activity. If you like golf, bring a putting green, putter, and some golf balls. Have your MC let the guests know that the longer the putt they sink, the better caliber of kiss

you will have to share to reward them. Your MC can randomly select guests to participate from a list compiled during your planning process. Or you can make your bridesmaids and groomsmen compete against each other. You can end the putting contest with a bride and groom putt-off to see who can sink the longest putt. A fun song to play during this activity could be 'I'm Alright' by Kenny Loggins. The same idea can apply using a mini basketball hoop with a mini basketball. The longest shot gets the best kiss. Another crowd favorite is Baggo, the beanbag toss game. I call it Wedding Baggo. It never ceases to amaze me how much noise the guests will make when one of the guests sinks a beanbag in the hole from 20 feet away."

CURTIS & AMY

MARCH 4, 2005
SCOTTSDALE, ARIZONA

The Return of the Damooko Brothers!

Long before Curtis and Amy first met, Curtis and his buddies used to go out to the nightclubs dressed up as the fictional, infamous "Damooko Brothers." Just for fun, during the garter removal and toss, the "Damooko Brothers" made one more public appearance, much to the joy and satisfaction of the ladies in attendance, including Amy.

* DINNER

Curtis and Amy chose a buffet dinner service and selected table names based on fun song titles that matched the people seated there (for example, Amy's family was seated at the "We Are Family" table). The guests were told to wait until their table song was playing before they could get in the line. When a table finally heard their song, many of them sang and danced their way over to the buffet line.

RECEPTION AGENDA

5:30–6:40
Drinks & Appetizers

6:40
Grand Entrance
"The Way You Move"
by OutKast

6:50
First Dance
"My Love"
by Lionel Richie

7:00–7:45
* Dinner

7:45
Toasts

8:00–8:30
Open Dancing

8:30
Cake Cutting
"I Can't Help Myself"
by Four Tops
"Sugar, Sugar"
by The Archies

8:45
Money Dance

9:00–9:20
Open Dancing

9:20
Bouquet & Garter Toss
"Lady Marmalade"
from Moulin Rouge Sdtk
"Play That Funky Music"
by Wild Cherry

9:30–10:25
Open Dancing

10:25
Last Dance
"At Last"
by Etta James
"Someone Like You"
by Van Morrison
"Let's Get It On"
by Marvin Gaye

Mike Anderson, a Wedding Entertainment Director from Minneapolis, has another idea. "For a couple who likes racing, set up a Hot Wheels track from the front edge of the head table down to the floor. Use a release box at the starting point and a finish line box with a lockout flag at the finish line. And finally, bring a collection of Hot Wheel racer cars. The tables select one couple per table to be their 'racer' and then the MC invites the racers up to the head table one couple at a time. They select a car from the box of cars and place it on the track next to the bride and groom's car. The cars are raced. If the bride and groom's car wins, the 'racer' couple has to share a kiss. If the 'racer' couple's car wins, the bride and groom have to kiss."

And here's one more example. Wedding Entertainment Director Mitch Taylor of Gladstone, Michigan, says: "One of my couples loved the Plinko game made popular on the game show *The Price Is Right*. The bride's father built a Plinko board, painted it red, and installed pegs in the usual diagonal pattern. He created eight landing slots at the bottom, four of which had the letters K-I-S-S painted on, with the four slots in between left blank. He called it 'Kiss Plinko' and the guests were given Ping-Pong balls to drop in the top. If their ball landed on the K, I, or either of the S slots, the bride and groom rewarded them with a kiss."

SINGING FOR THEIR DINNER ★★★★

When it's time to invite your guests to join the buffet line, ask your MC to instruct them that they cannot get in the line until they have serenaded you with a song that includes the word "love." They will be expected to sing to you as a group in front of your table. Then, and only then, will they be invited to get in the line. (Note that a band may not be able to stop playing to accommodate the guests' singing as easily as a DJ can fade down the background music.)

SONG TITLES FOR TABLE NAMES WITH A BUFFET ★★★★★

Name your guests' tables based on song titles. The titles can reflect a theme or be used as a "label" of sorts for the guests at each table. When it's time to invite your guests to join the buffet line, have your MC instruct them that they will know they are the next to get in line when their table's corresponding song is played. At a reception in Silverado Canyon, the bride and groom, who had met at a George Strait music festival, named their tables after their favorite George Strait songs.

BRIDE AND GROOM BUFFET LINE TRIVIA ★★★★

Curtis Hoekstra, a Wedding Entertainment Director based in Phoenix, says, "Ask your MC to advise your guests that they will be expected to show how much they know about the two of you. They must correctly answer random trivia questions about you before they can get in the buffet line. To keep too many people from guessing at once, they will need to raise their hand only when they are sure they have the answer. If they get the answer wrong, they will have to point to a different table, which will be sent to the buffet line ahead of them as a consequence. When done correctly, your guests will be completely entertained while waiting for their turn to go eat." The band may need to take a break while the MC directs this activity.

ARE YOU SMARTER THAN THE WEDDING PARTY? ★★★★★

"Following the example of the game show *Are You Smarter Than A Fifth Grader?*" says Dallas-based Wedding Entertainment Director Chad Alan Wandel, "one of my engaged couples, who are both teachers, asked if we could create an adaptation. To get the buffet line started, I asked a random trivia question to one table at a time. Before the question was posed, the table was asked to pick which wedding party member they would like to challenge. Once the question was asked, the table was given 20 seconds to deliberate for a final answer, which they were to write on a large index card with a large Sharpie pen. Then I asked the chosen wedding party member to answer the question. If that person gave the correct answer and the table got it right as well, we played another round. If the wedding party member gave the correct answer and the table got it wrong, the table was told to point out a table that would get be the next in line for the buffet. If the wedding party member gave the wrong answer and the table got it right, then the table was

invited to get in the line. If the wedding party member and the table both gave the wrong answer, the first new table to jump up and give the correct answer gets to be invited to join the buffet."

BUFFET LINE NAME THAT TUNE ****

"Test your guests' music knowledge by having your MC get them to 'Name That Tune,' suggests Sacramento-based Wedding Entertainment Director Doug LaVine. "The first person to correctly identify the song being played by your band or DJ will earn his table's chance to get in the buffet line. Songs that have the word 'love' in the title can be fun. Instrumental (such as Vitamin String Quartet) versions of popular current hits can really keep your guests guessing. Selections from Paul Anka's 'Rock Swings' album can also keep them on their toes."

BUFFET LINE REVERSE NAME THAT TUNE *****

Chad Alan Wandel of Dallas adds a twist to the "name that tune" idea. "Using audio editing software, your DJ can prepare a collection of popular songs that have been 'flipped' so they will play backwards. The first table to correctly identify the song while it is playing backwards will earn their table's chance to get in the buffet line. Then the DJ can play a short clip of the song in the normal format to confirm that their answer was correct."

SPEED DIAL YOUR WAY TO THE BUFFET LINE *****

Larry Williams, a Wedding Entertainment Director based in Reno, submitted the following creative buffet line activity. "The MC will invite the guests to appoint one person at each table who has a cell phone as their table's official 'dialer.' The MC will give out the phone number of either the bride or groom's cell phone with strict instructions not to dial until his hand is dropped. When the MC drops his hand, the official dialers begin frantically dialing while the guests at their tables cheer them on. The first dialer to get through will earn their table's chance to get in the buffet line. To add even more to this event, the dialers can be asked to take a photo of the cake, the centerpieces, the gift table, etc. and then text it to the phone number. The first photo to get through is the winner."

WRITING AND RECITING POETRY FOR THEIR DINNER ✳✳✳✳

Shawn Whittemore, a Wedding Entertainment Director from Lake Oswego, Oregon, suggests, "Arrange for a piece of paper and a pencil to be placed on each table in advance of the meal. Ask your MC to instruct the guests at each table to work together as a team to write a poem about the two of you. The first table that can stand and read their completed poem aloud will be the first to get in line for the buffet. The MC will collect each of the poems after they have been read aloud so they can later be added to a scrapbook."

ROCK, PAPER, SCISSORS FOR THE BUFFET LINE ✳✳✳✳

Alex Tamas, a Wedding Entertainment Director in Victoria, British Columbia, shares, "During a planning session with one of my couples, it became apparent they enjoyed playing Rock, Paper, Scissors when it came to resolving who gets to use the remote control. When it came time to decide how the tables were going to be invited to the buffet line, I suggested using this game as an alternative. Each table was asked to select a table captain. Two table captains were called up to compete head to head. The winner's table earned the next spot in the buffet line. The losing captain had to play against the next randomly selected table, and continued to do so until finally winning. The couple loved it, and it was a huge success."

BRIDE OR GROOM? ✳✳✳✳✳

Chad Alan Wandel has another buffet line activity suggestion. "This activity requires a collection of pictures of the bride and groom. Before you play the game, you will need to set up PowerPoint slides for the game. This is done by creating two slides for every picture. On the first slide you zoom into a feature of the image where it is hard to tell who it is or perhaps it just looks funny. Then you ask a table if this is the bride or the groom. After they answer, click to the next slide and have the image scale out to normal size to find out the answer. This can be very amusing, especially if you get some funny pictures. However, the setup for this activity requires a projector, screen, and someone to operate the PowerPoint slides. This isn't something that can be done on the spur of the moment."

"BE OUR GUEST" CATERING STAFF INTRODUCTION ✳✳✳

If the catering staff would like to join in on the fun, have your MC formally announce them into the room while playing "Be Our Guest" from the soundtrack of Disney's *Beauty & The Beast* (or "Hot Hot Hot" by Buster Poindexter). Then the catering staff comes out and lines up shoulder to shoulder facing your guests. Or they might serve the head table their first entrée in dramatic fashion. They might even be carrying plates topped with fancy silver covers. One location in Orange County, California, regularly does this at the beginning of its sit-down meals. Check with your caterer to make sure your MC fully understands the music and timing issues involved.

DO A CENTERPIECE GIVEAWAY ACTIVITY **/*****

If the centerpieces on the guest tables can be taken home as keepsakes, consider using a centerpiece giveaway activity to create some fun energy that will leave your guests laughing and/or cheering. These ideas can range from simple to complex, from humorous to energetic, or from generic to highly personalized. They can also serve as ice breakers to help the guests get to know each other at their tables, or just to inject some great energy into the mealtime. Here are some examples:

WHO HAS THE WINNING CHAIR? **/***

Place a sticker underneath one chair per table and then invite your guests to turn their chairs over in search of the hidden sticker. This can be expanded by having them walk around the table, moving from chair to chair as the music plays. When the music suddenly stops, they turn over the chair that's currently in front of them. Let your MC know that you want to do this activity and make sure the chairs are not already "labeled" from a previous event. Multiple stickers per table would certainly confuse the guests.

CLOSEST BIRTHDAY, FARTHEST TRAVELED, ETC. **/***

Ask the guests to compare specific information about themselves at their own table. Then ask for the one person at each table to stand who has the following: a birthday closest to your wedding date; traveled the farthest; known the bride and groom the longest; etc. They could then be introduced as the winner, or you could ask them to congratulate the person to their right as the winner, resulting in a wave of laughter from the guests.

PENNIES FROM HEAVEN **/*****

Put a penny under one bread plate per table, and then invite your guests to lift their bread plates to discover who has already won. For a sit-down meal, be sure to schedule this event to take place before the salad course is completed, as the catering staff will commonly remove the bread plates along with the salad plates. If the MC begins too late, there may no longer be any bread plates to lift up and the pennies will already be in plain view. I share this advice from firsthand experience. At a fabulous reception in New Jersey, I found myself in this exact predicament.

With a little ingenuity, I was able to still use the pennies as a trick that convinced most of the guests that they had just magically appeared.

THE NAPKIN PASS ***/*****

While some music plays, have the guests pass around a linen napkin at the table, waving it over their heads as it goes by. When the music stops, the person with the napkin is the winner. Or that person can be asked to fold the napkin and drape it over his left arm as he has now been appointed as the table's waiter and will be responsible for fetching the table's drinks…right after he congratulates the real centerpiece winner on his left.

THE DOLLAR PASS ***/*****

Have one person per table volunteer to hold up a one dollar bill, which will be passed around the table as the music plays. When the music stops, the person with the dollar will think he is the winner, and he might be if you so choose. But you could tell him that he has won second prize and gets to keep the dollar. The person who lost his dollar is then identified as having "purchased" the centerpiece.

ROCK, PAPER, SCISSORS FOR THE CENTERPIECE ***/*****

Have your MC identify two people per table and ask them to stand. They can be the person at the table who traveled the farthest and the person who came the shortest distance. They can be the person at the table who has known either the bride and groom the longest and shortest amount of time. Other options can be used. Once these two people per table have been identified and are standing, the MC will let them know that they will be competing for the centerpiece by playing Rock, Paper, Scissors. Paper covers Rock and wins. Rock smashes Scissors and wins. And Scissors cuts Paper and wins.

WORDS OF WISDOM CARDS *****

Using the "Words of Wisdom Cards" idea from Chapter 14, have the guests fill out one note card per person at their tables. Once the cards are completed, have the guests share their answers at their table and then select the one card with the funniest or most creative advice as the winner. The winning cards will then be read aloud by the MC in an entertaining way toward the end of the meal.

FIRST BABY NAME CARDS *****

Another twist on the "Words of Wisdom Cards" is "First Baby Name Cards." If neither of you has any children yet, and you are planning on starting a family someday (and/or the groom's last name could create some fun suggestions, such as Barbee, Dickey, Haze), have the guests fill out one card per person with one fun and creative first baby name. Once the note cards are completed, have the guests at each table share their answers and then select the card with the funniest or most creative baby name as the winner. The winning cards will be entertainingly read aloud by the MC near the end of the meal.

YOUR OWN PERSONAL "TOP 10" LIST *****

Randy Bartlett, a nationally known DJ trainer and Wedding Entertainment Director based in Sacramento, says, "Invite your guests to create a David Letterman–style Top 10 list about the two of you. Have them create ten fun endings to the line 'The Top 10 Reasons Why Joe and Sally Should Be Together are…' as a table. Then the best ten lines from all the tables will be selected, compiled, and presented for everyone to hear by the MC at the end of the meal." It is vital that your MC can compile the best order based on humor and can confidently deliver the punch lines.

RSVP SPOTLIGHT *****

Keep track of the first five or more guests (singles, couples, families) to send in their RSVP cards and give their names to your MC. Near the end of the meal, have your

Gauging an MC's Level of Skill & Talent

You may have noticed that several of the ideas in this chapter have been scored on a sliding scale (i.e., 2 to 5 stars). These rating ranges were created because depending on how skilled and/or knowledgeable your MC is with the added enhancements (such as creative punch lines or the timing of the punch lines), he may only be able to deliver the simplest version. Use these suggestions as a test. Ask the MC how he is able to turn these activities into 5-star events. But don't give him all the details. His answers may tell you quite a bit about his skill level as a wedding entertainer. Also, be sure to request video footage, as the MC may be able to describe it better than he can deliver. This test could help you find the best MC for your reception's entertainment needs.

MC invite these unwitting guests up to the dance floor to receive some kind of surprise recognition. Playing a mysterious sounding theme in the background can really add to the moment. Challenge the other guests to guess what these people have done to be deserving of whatever honor they are about to receive. As the audience gets involved by throwing out their queries, the MC will finally reveal the real answer and will present them with a small gift, like a box of chocolates or a gift card from a favorite store.

LOTTERY SCRATCHER GUEST FAVORS ****

Put an envelope with enough lottery scratcher tickets for each guest at the table under each table's centerpiece. Have your MC inform your guests to find the envelope and pass out the tickets without scratching them. When instructed, all of the guests will scratch off their tickets at the same time, and random shouts from cash prize winners will be heard from different seats in the room. Perhaps your band or DJ could play "Luck Be A Lady" by Frank Sinatra to add a little bit more fun.

FUTURE ANNIVERSARY CARDS ***

Place an anniversary card, all with different years of marriage assigned on the envelope, along with a pen on each guest table. Include printed instructions (so the MC won't spoil the surprise by announcing it) that will ask the guests at each table to sign the card and write a note they would like the two of you to read on that particular anniversary. Once the cards are completed and sealed, they will be collected and put with the regular gift cards, so the bride and groom can discover them later. On many of their future anniversaries, the bride and groom will be able to open yet another anniversary card that will bring back fond memories of their wedding day.

MAKE A TIME CAPSULE ***

James Loram, a popular Southern California wedding entertainer, says, "Place note cards and pens at each table and provide your MC with a small, steel canister to be used as a time capsule. Have the MC invite the guests to fill out the cards with their names and some special thoughts to share with the bride and groom. The MC will collect all of the cards and any other fun mementos the guests may want to include. These will be sealed inside the steel container until their first, tenth, or even twenty-fifth anniversary."

CHAPTER 18
THE SPECIAL DANCES

*W*hen your first dance begins, your guests will certainly be watching. Some
will be remembering when they shared their own first dance. Others
might be picturing how they'll look when they finally share their own first
dance. But for the two of you, the world may feel like it has suddenly slowed to half
speed as you find yourselves lost in each other's eyes. The moment is only broken by
full smiles and laughter as your husband (that's right, he's your husband now) says
to you, "Can you believe it? We're really married now!" Unfortunately, some special
dances can be given less than special treatment by entertainment vendors who may
have forgotten how truly meaningful, personal, and emotional these dances should be.
In this chapter, we will consider several unique ways to turn your special dances into
truly unforgettable moments.

TURN ON THE BUBBLE MACHINE **

My grandmother used to make me watch *The Lawrence Welk Show* with her. My
favorite moment was when the bubbles began to fill the studio's dance floor. I
don't actually recommend using a bubble machine, even though it can provide a
dramatic effect. Instead, invite your guests to gather around the dance floor with
small bottles of bubbles and ask them to be your bubble machine. Your guests
will enjoy being more involved in your celebration and you'll get some really cute
photos with bubbles in the air and your smiling guests as the backdrop. When you
shop for the bubbles, look for "nonslip" bubbles so your dance floor won't become
slippery.

YOU LIGHT UP MY LIFE ***/*****

Ben Miller, a Wedding Entertainment Director in Illinois, says, "There are high-tech
and low-tech lighting effects that can enhance your first dance in truly creative

ways. Using specialized lighting, you can dance under a bright spotlight as the room is darkened. You might even choose to have your monogram or your names projected in lights that slowly spin about the room. Be sure the entertainment vendor you choose has the right equipment and expertise to create these effects properly. For a more low-tech approach, provide everyone with votive candles or sparklers to light and hold as they gather around the dance floor during your first dance. Not only will your guests enjoy being more involved in your celebration, but you'll get some striking photos. Make sure your MC knows this will be happening so the guests can be reminded ahead of time to get their candles or sparklers ready and lit. Always check this out with your reception location in advance because of possible fire hazard issues. And it's always wise to test your candles or sparklers before buying a large quantity, to see which ones will last the longest and will give off the least amount of smoke. Finally, provide two or three sparklers per guest and have the MC instruct them to use the sparklers only one at a time, so they will last throughout your entire first dance."

DANCING ON THE CLOUDS *****

"Would you like to create the illusion that the two of you are dancing on top of the clouds?" asks Wedding Entertainment Director Mike Anderson. "Using the latest in theatrical stage fog technology, combined with specialized lighting effects, an entertainment company with the right tools and qualifications can create this amazing fairytale setting come true." You can see a video of this effect in action on Mike's Web site, www.creativememoriesdj.com/tbwreclouds.html. This overall effect is very dramatic, but also very complicated to create. Your entertainment company must have a thorough understanding about the proper use of the equipment needed.

DANCING UNDER FALLING SNOWFLAKES *****

Mike Anderson also recommends another breathtaking special effect for your first dance. "Imagine sharing your first dance underneath gently falling snowflakes. With the right snow machine, this fantasy moment can become reality and the pictures will be truly amazing." Watch a video of this effect on Mike's Web site, http://www.creativememoriesdj.com/tbwresnow.html. It is very dramatic, but also complicated to create. Your entertainment company will need a thorough understanding about the proper use of the equipment to make this effect turn out correctly. Do not attempt this without testing whether the snowflakes can cause slippage.

CHOREOGRAPHED FIRST DANCE *****

If the idea of your approaching first dance is making you nervous, consider the possibility that some simple dance lessons might help. As your comfort and confidence grow during your classes, perhaps you will feel ready to do a little bit more, like creating your own special first dance routine. This can be especially memorable if one or both of you is not commonly known as a dancer. When the music begins and you suddenly put on an amazing show, your guests will not be able to contain their surprise and admiration. Check out "Chip & Deanna's First Dance with a Twist" (http://www.youtube.com/tbwre#p/u/9/tbt1d7ZiVls). Chip and Deanna's routine was very well rehearsed and highly innovative and had a terrific impact on their guests. Make sure your MC knows you want to do this and has worked out your music cues.

RECORD A SPECIAL MESSAGE *****

One way to enhance the emotional impact of your special dances is to record a special message that can either precede the song or be mixed into the song during the instrumental segments. If you both record messages separately and then have your MC mix them into your first dance song, it will not only make your dance more personalized and memorable, but it can also be a nice romantic surprise. You will both get to hear the other's words of affection for the very first time on the dance floor. This idea can be added to the other dances as well. One bride had selected an unusual song for her father/daughter dance. When I pressed her for more information about the selection, she revealed that when she was little her dad would read books and sing songs to her, and "Joy To The World" by Three Dog Night was the song she remembered most of all. So whenever she hears that song she thinks about her father. We recorded her voice giving that explanation, which played over the song's introduction and brought a tear to her dad's eye, just before he started laughing as the lyrics, "Jeremiah was a bullfrog…" played over the speakers. Another great example of this idea can be seen in Eric and Rebecca's profile (opposite page). It is very important that your MC fully understands how to do this properly so it won't be presented poorly. He will need strong audio editing skills to create edits that are both technically superior as well as emotionally powerful. Ask him to share some previous examples of his special recordings and mixes to gauge his skill levels in this area.

NEW PARENTS DANCE **

James Loram, a popular wedding entertainer based in Fullerton, California, says, "Why not add a new twist to the traditional father/daughter and mother/son dances? Take a moment to spotlight your new parents by inviting the groom's father to dance with the bride and the bride's mother to dance with the groom."

ADD A VIDEO MONTAGE *** /*****

Wedding Entertainment Director Ben Miller suggests, "To add an extra special touch to your first dance, the father/daughter dance, and/or the mother/son dance, consider putting together a video montage slideshow featuring photos of the bride and groom together in the various stages of their relationship, or photos of the bride and her father or the groom and his mother through their growing-up years. If either the bride or the groom would prefer less attention during their special dances, showing a video montage might relieve some of that concern." You can see a video of this effect on Ben's Web site (http://www.thepremierproductions.com/index.php/entertainment/photo-slideshows/).

ERIC & REBECCA

JANUARY 8, 2006
LAGUNA BEACH, CALIFORNIA

A Mother/Son Dance to Remember

Eric wanted to dance with his mom to "You Are My Sunshine" because she had taught him to sing the chorus when he was a little boy. His mother sent me an old cassette that she suggested might help the guests understand why the song was so special to them. The tape had Eric's voice on it, singing the chorus of "You Are My Sunshine" when he was just three years old! We made a special edit featuring Eric's adorable little voice singing over the instrumental portion. In the end, they were both surprised and there wasn't a dry eye in sight.

* FIRST DANCE

Eric and Rebecca wanted to have fun with their first dance. About a minute into their song, it came to an abrupt halt but immediately transitioned into one of their favorite upbeat numbers. Their guests enjoyed this creative twist.

RECEPTION AGENDA

2:00
Grand Entrance
"Christmas Eve Sarajevo"
by Trans-Siberian Orchestra

2:10
* First Dance
"The Nearness Of You"
by Norah Jones
"I'm On My Way"
by The Proclaimers

2:15–3:20
Toasts, Dinner & Dances
Father/Daughter Dance
"The Way You Look Tonight"
by Steve Tyrell
Mother/Son Dance
"You Are My Sunshine"
by Bing Crosby
**Parents &
Wedding Party Dance**
"Through The Eyes Of Love"
by Melissa Manchester
Longevity Dance
"Young At Heart"
by Frank Sinatra

3:20–3:45
Open Dancing

3:45
Cake Cutting
"Knock Me A Kiss"
by Louis Jordan
"I Got You Babe"
by Sonny & Cher

4:00
Bouquet & Garter Toss
"American Woman"
by Lenny Kravitz
"I Need A Man" by Eurythmics
"I'm A Loser" by The Beatles
"Minnie The Moocher"
by Big Bad Voodoo Daddy
"Who Let The Dogs Out"
by Baha Men

4:10–4:55
Open Dancing

4:55
Last Dance
"True Companion" by Marc Cohn

WEDDING PARTY DANCE/ DANCE CONTEST ***

Turn the typically slow wedding party dance into a dance contest by selecting a fast song that your wedding party will all enjoy. Then form a circle and see who jumps in the middle to show off their smooth moves. Or form two lines facing each other, with bridesmaids on one side and groomsmen on the other as they rotate couples down the middle, between the lines, while displaying their best fancy footwork. Some may refer to this as a "Soul Train." This is also commonly referred to as a "Grand March" in the upper Midwest and can easily turn into a snowball dance, or the guests can be invited to join in on the fun partway through.

INVITE OTHERS TO JOIN IN ***

If you are truly uncomfortable sharing your entire first dance all by yourselves, invite your wedding party members to join in with you after a minute or so. During the father/daughter dance and/or the mother/son dance, your MC could invite any other fathers and daughters or mothers and sons to join you on the dance floor. If the bride has both a father and a stepfather, and she has a close relationship with both of them, perhaps the MC could invite the stepfather to cut in halfway through the father/ daughter dance. During your wedding party dance, your MC could invite the rest of the guests to join in halfway through in an effort to lead into the open dancing. They could be invited up by staggered categories, such as immediate family, out-of-state guests, local guests, etc. Make sure your MC knows you want to invite others to join and knows the timing you would prefer for making such invitations.

THE LONGEVITY/ ANNIVERSARY DANCE ****

This special dance creates an opportunity for you to honor, acknowledge, and even seek some free marital advice from the longest married couple in attendance. It can be done in a variety of ways. One method involves inviting all of the married couples to join you for

JUNE 30, 2007
ORANGE, CALIFORNIA

Shock & Awe!

Doug and Jesse created a moment that their guests will certainly never forget. As their first dance song started to skip in the middle of their dance, their guests began to gasp. But when a mix of upbeat songs started to play and they began pulling off a fun choreographed dance routine, their friends and family gave them a loud standing ovation. Their videographer captured it all and you can watch it here: (http://www.youtube.com/watch?v=XKCO8aIxG2Q).

* LAST DANCE

Doug and Jesse opted for Queen's "Bohemian Rhapsody" as their last dance song selection. Because the song is not great for dancing, we brought out a cordless microphone and invited their guests to circle up and sing along.

RECEPTION AGENDA

6:00–7:05
Drinks & Appetizers

7:05
Grand Entrance
"Thunderstruck"
by AC/DC

7:15
Toasts

7:30–8:30
Dinner

8:30–8:50
The Special Dances
Father/Daughter Dance
"Daughters"
by John Mayer
Mother/Son Dance
"In My Life"
by The Beatles
First Dance
"Can't Help Falling In Love"
by Elvis Presley

8:50–9:15
Open Dancing

9:15
Cake Cutting
"Sugar, Sugar"
by The Archies

9:30
Money Dance

9:50–10:00
Bouquet & Garter Toss
"American Woman"
by Lenny Kravitz
"Man! I Feel Like A Woman"
by Shania Twain
"I'm A Loser"
by The Beatles
"Oh Yeah"
by Yello
"The Benny Hill Show Theme"
by Boots Randolph

10:00–12:00 (a.m.)
Open Dancing

12:00 (a.m.)
* Last Dance
"Bohemian Rhapsody"
by Queen

a special dance in honor of marriage. The music starts and during the course of the song the married couples are invited to take their seats based on years of marriage accrued, starting with the two of you and building up towards whoever has been married the longest. As the couples on the dance floor begin to thin out, there will soon be just one couple left. Your guests will naturally begin to applaud. At this point, your MC could take a moment to introduce them by name and years of marriage, and maybe even ask them to briefly share their secret for staying married so long. At one of my receptions, the last couple had been married for fifty-three years. When I asked them how to stay married that long, the husband's response was, "Don't die!" Because this method results in an empty dance floor, it might be best to schedule it to take place just before a slower event, like the cake cutting, the money dance/dollar dance, or the next course of the meal.

Another approach is to wait to start the song until the couple married the longest has first been identified by simply moving the couples across the dance floor, from one side to the other, by ascending years of marriage. Once the couple married the longest has been revealed (they are the last couple standing on one side of the floor), all the married couples are invited to dance, which can create a segue into your open dancing. After all, your dance floor will most likely be filled with married couples at this point. If the longest married couple is not mobile enough to participate, this activity can be done during the meal as a "Longevity/Anniversary Spotlight." Between courses or after the buffet line has cleared, have all the couples stand up. Then begin having them sit back down based on years of marriage accrued, starting with the two of you and building up towards whoever has been married the longest, who can then be introduced by your MC.

CHAPTER 19

THE CAKE CUTTING

*C*utting a cake has been a traditional part of wedding celebrations for literally thousands of years. It started as a symbol of fertility, with the husband break-ing a wheat cake over his new wife's head to represent that he was ready to start a family and was hopeful that she would give him many children. The guests would clamor to eat the falling crumbs, which were believed to bring good luck. In the sixteenth century, wedding cakes began to be served in layers with a delicious frosting. And today, it is commonly seen as your first official meal as husband and wife. Wheth-er you serve each other gently, or give in to your guests' cajoling and treat each other to a faceful of frosting, this is one of those moments your guests won't want to miss. Here are some fun ways to get your guests a little more involved.

HAVE YOUR GUESTS SERENADE YOU ****

Your MC can pass out lyric sheets to the guests just before your cake cutting and then invite everyone to gather around the cake and sing a song to the two of you while you cut your cake and feed each other. There are several great songs that can be lots of fun: "That's Amoré" by Dean Martin, "I Got You Babe" by Sonny & Cher, or "How Sweet It Is (To Be Loved By You)" by Marvin Gaye. If your MC tells your guests this idea is a surprise, you'll likely get even more participation because everyone likes helping with a surprise. Be sure your MC knows that you want to do this, has the lyric sheets ready, and is prepared to help set it up properly.

CONGA LINE TO THE CAKE ****

Mark "Peace" Thomas, a Wedding Entertainment Director based in Canyon Lake, California, suggests, "In an effort to move smoothly from the open dancing to the cake cutting while also trying to gather as many guests around to watch as the bride and groom cut their cake, we created a conga line towards the end of the open dancing that attracted most of the guests to join in. Once they were following the bride and groom around the room to 'Conga' by Gloria Estefan, the bride and groom led the line over to their cake. They arrived with the majority of their guests in tow and then we announced the cake cutting. Over 90 percent of their guests were already gathered to watch as the bride and groom cut their cake and fed each other."

THE CAKE SMASH WITH A SNEAK ATTACK ****

Invite your best man and maid/matron of honor to join you for a posed picture at the cake to recreate the formal cake-cutting photos from the 1940s and earlier. This explanation is merely a ruse that your MC can use to get them into position for what's about to happen next. Just as you're about to feed each other, and your guests are encouraging you to smash the cake, pull a fast one and smash cake on their faces. Your MC and your photographer should be informed in advance that you want to do this so they can help you pull it off without your best man or maid/matron of honor getting suspicious.

KYLE & CASEY

FEBRUARY 14, 2009
TEMECULA, CALIFORNIA

The Valentine's Day Themed Cake

Kyle and Casey chose to get married on Valentine's Day because they are both very romantic. They designed their wedding cake with a Valentine's Day heart theme. We made a "no cake smashing" promo announcement to remind them to stay romantic instead of giving into the demands of their guests, who, of course, were cheering for them to get "caked."

* BOUQUET & GARTER TOSS

Kyle and Casey wanted to add a little more incentive for their guests to participate in their bouquet and garter tosses. Instead of calling up only the single people, we invited all of their guests to join in. The woman who caught the bouquet received a gift card for Victoria's Secret and the gentleman who caught the garter was presented with a gift card for Best Buy.

RECEPTION AGENDA

5:10–6:15
Drinks & Appetizers

6:15
Grand Entrance
"Flashing Lights"
by Kanye West

6:25
Toasts

6:40–7:50
Dinner

7:50
Video Montage

8:00
Cake Cutting
"Sugar, Sugar" by The Archies
"Pour Some Sugar On Me"
by Def Leppard

8:25–8:40
The Special Dances
First Dance
"The First Time"
by James Burns
Father/Daughter Dance
"Fly Little Bluebird"
by James Burns
Mother/Son Dance
"The Perfect Fan"
by Backstreet Boys

8:40–9:20
Open Dancing

9:20
* Bouquet & Garter Toss
"Material Girl"
by Madonna
"Express Yourself"
by Madonna
"You Shook Me
All Night Long" by AC/DC
"I Touch Myself"
by The Divinyls
"I'm Shipping Up To Boston"
by Dropkick Murphys

9:30–10:30
Open Dancing

10:30
Last Dance
"Dancing In The Moonlight"
by King Harvest

HAVE THE BRIDESMAIDS PULL CAKE CHARMS ****

Cake charms are small silver charms that are baked into the cake with strings attached. Prior to the cake cutting, these charms can be pulled from the cake by the bridesmaids and/or the single ladies in attendance. The charms are supposed to represent what may lie in store for each bridesmaid who retrieves one. For example, the four-leaf clover charm represents good luck, the anchor charm represents a life of stability, and the sailboat charm represents a life of adventure and travel. Make sure your MC knows how to properly introduce the significance of the cake charms.

PROVIDE A CREATIVE "GROOM'S CAKE" ***

In the South and Midwest, it is fairly common to have a groom's cake in addition to the formal wedding cake. Often this cake is chocolate covered with chocolate frosting and chocolate-covered strawberries, or more commonly it is a themed cake. In the movie *Steel Magnolias*, the groom's cake was shaped and decorated as an armadillo. I have seen groom's cakes shaped like a surfboard on a wave, a tuxedo, and a cowboy boot. At one reception, the groom, who was from New York, chose a cake shaped like a Yankees baseball cap. We played some Yankees theme music when the cake was presented. Make sure your MC knows you will be having a groom's cake and is prepared to explain its significance, if necessary.

HONOR SOMEONE'S BIRTHDAY/ANNIVERSARY ***

If one of your guests in attendance will be celebrating a birthday or a special anniversary on your wedding day, have the MC invite him to join you at the cake table so you can present him with the second slice. If it's a birthday, perhaps you could put a lit candle in the slice of cake and invite everyone to sing "Happy Birthday." Be sure your MC will be aware that this is going to happen and will be prepared to make an introduction.

PROVIDE "TABLE CAKES" ***

Minneapolis-based Wedding Entertainment Director Bill Hermann suggests, "Have your baker make individual cakes to be set as the centerpieces on each of the guest tables. Before you cut your own smaller, formal cake at the cake table (or on your

CHRIS & LAUREN

SEPTEMBER 15, 2007
MONARCH BEACH, CALIFORNIA

The Cake Chopping?

Because he works as a firefighter, Chris and Lauren decided to cut their wedding cake with a highly polished fireman's axe. They also arranged for an ice block to be carved into the shape of a fire engine, which then served as an "ice luge" for serving martinis at the bar.

* CRAZY IN LOVE

Chris and Lauren's first dance song was a romantic, slow song. But as the song was ending, it suddenly mixed into the fast song, "Crazy In Love" by Beyoncé, and their wedding party members rushed out onto the dance floor to cut loose with them. All their guests began applauding loudly.

own table), the MC will ask the guests to select one couple per table who they consider the most romantic couple of their group. The MC will then invite each of these 'romantic couples' to stand. At the same time, each of the couples, along with the bride and groom, will cut their table's cake, serve the first slice onto the plate, feed each other, and then kiss. When they are done, the guests will be invited to cut up and serve their own cakes at each table." Be sure your MC is aware that this is going to happen and will be prepared to properly instruct your guests when the time comes.

CUPCAKES INSTEAD OF A CAKE **

At a recent reception, the bride and groom replaced the traditional wedding cake with a pyramid display of creatively decorated cupcakes. When the time came for the traditional cake cutting, the bride and groom sank their teeth into one shared cupcake from opposite sides. Then their guests were invited to come collect their own cupcakes for dessert.

BRING IN A CHOCOLATE FOUNTAIN **

In lieu of a cake, perhaps melted chocolate is more to your liking. Your guests will find the chocolate aroma irresistible. Add an assorted collection of brownies, marshmallows, Rice Krispie treats, Oreo cookies, banana slices, pineapple chunks, and

other tasty items for dipping, and your guests will enjoy a very entertaining dessert. If your location doesn't offer a chocolate fountain as a dessert option, there may be a local rental company in your area that can provide it as well as the chocolate and items for dipping.

CREATE AN ICE CREAM SUNDAE BAR **

One bride and groom decided to forgo the traditional cake cutting and hosted an ice cream sundae bar instead. With a variety of toppings to choose from, the guests were able to create their own sundaes to enjoy for dessert. The guests also enjoyed watching the bride and groom feed each other from a sundae they had created together.

BUILD A CANDY BUFFET **

To give their guests some creative options for satisfying a sweet tooth, one bride and groom arranged a buffet table of assorted candy treats (such as M&Ms, Sweet Tarts, Hershey Kisses, red licorice, and sugar-covered fruit slices) with scoops and containers.

CREATE A DESSERT COURSE PLAYLIST ***

New Jersey wedding entertainer Mike Walter says, "Ask your band or DJ to put together a fun playlist of songs as a perfect soundtrack for the dessert course as the cake is being served. A few popular suggestions are: 'Sugar, Sugar' by The Archies, 'Sugar Shack' by Jerry Gilmer, 'Sweetest Thing' by U2, 'I Want Candy' by Bow Wow Wow, and 'The Candy Man" by Sammy Davis, Jr."

CHAPTER 20

THE MONEY DANCE/DOLLAR DANCE

ome brides have been known to spend upwards of $10,000 for a Vera Wang bridal gown. Floral centerpieces for twenty guest tables can easily average $500 or more. But what's the value of giving your guests a chance to dance and connect with you, one on one, during your wedding reception? Some would say, PRICELESS! The most common misperception about the money dance/dollar dance is that your guests will see it as the two of you begging for honeymoon spending cash. However, in my experience, that couldn't be further from the truth. If you are uncomfortable with this event, then don't do it. In this chapter, however, we'll discuss some options that remove the reference to money altogether, as well as a few ways to make it even more enjoyable.

REGULATE THE LINES ***

If you have a large guest count (200 or more), your money dance could drag on too long and start to have a negative impact. Ask your best man and maid/matron of honor to help regulate the lines of people who are waiting for their turn to dance with you. Sending in a new person every 45 seconds or even sooner can keep things moving at a steady pace. Be sure your MC knows this will be happening, so instructions on the timing can be given to your best man and maid/matron of honor.

THE QUICK-MIX MONEY DANCE/DOLLAR DANCE ****

Michigan-based Wedding Entertainment Director Mitch Taylor adds, "Have the best man and maid/matron of honor tell the next person in line to cut in whenever the song changes. Then, following your prior instructions, have your band or DJ segue or mix out of each song after 30–45 seconds. This will keep the lines moving at a decent pace."

BRING SAFETY PINS FOR THE GROOM **

When guests come up to dance with the groom, they'll be given safety pins so they can pin their greenbacks all over his tuxedo. Pretty soon the groom will be covered with cash, literally. Make sure your MC knows that safety pins will be used so the guests can be informed.

BRING YOUR OWN CREATIVE "PURSE" *

White satin purses for this event can be commonly found at bridal shops. But don't be afraid to come up with your own creative "purse." Your maid/matron of honor can hold a treasure chest or a large tip jar. Or bring an old white pillowcase with a big dollar sign printed on it.

DON'T CALL IT A MONEY DANCE/DOLLAR DANCE ****

Give the dance any name you want. Call it a special dance, a honeymoon dance, a congratulatory dance, etc. Have your MC announce it with no mention of the word "money" while instead putting the focus on how this will be an opportunity for your guests to offer their best wishes to you, one on one. Truth be told, even without

mentioning money, I have seen several of these "special dances" where a fair number of the guests still came up with money in hand. But the bride and groom were no longer uncomfortable because there had been no overt request for money. It is very important that your MC understands your wishes in this regard. Some MCs have a habit of making the same announcements at every wedding the same exact way, as if they are on autopilot.

RUN WITH THE "MONEY THEME"
****

Why not try having some fun with the dance? Instead of worrying about what your guests will think, have your MC invite them to bring up tens, twenties, and all major credit cards. Play "money-themed" musical selections and instruct the guests that they must dance with you in a style that matches the tempo of each song. Put a fundraiser thermometer on the wall with an outrageously high projected goal for the night.

Ask your MC to use your honeymoon destination along with a bad impression of a televangelist to make a plea for funds that sounds something like this: "Brothers and sisters-uh, I've had a vision from God-uh of these two lovely children enjoying a beautiful honeymoon-uh on the beaches of Hawaii-uh. But I'm sad to tell you that vision-uh will not become a reality-uh unless you are willing-uh to open up your purse strings-uh and give-uh. So right now-uh, I'm asking you-uh…I'm pleading with you-uh…to dig deep brothers and sisters-uh, so we can make sure this vision-uh become a reality-uh. They can accept all denominations-uh, and out of state checks-uh. And they'll even be more happy-uh to take your credit cards-uh."

Now I know that example was completely over the top. But you might be surprised to know that I actually used it at the specific request of a bride and groom who wanted to do something that was completely over the top. That was their style.

It fit them perfectly. What's your style? Be very clear with your MC about how you might want to run with the "money theme" at your reception. Be sure he can present your ideas appropriately as well.

THE DOLLAR PASS JUMP START ****

Building on the "Dollar Pass" idea from Chapter 17, Wedding Entertainment Director Ron Ruth says, "To get past the initial lull that can occur as we are waiting for the guests to begin forming lines for the money dance/dollar dance, why not use the dollar pass idea as a fun way to segue into this event? Then, when the dollar pass ends, the MC will instruct those who have been left holding the dollar to bring it to the dance floor as they have been selected for a special honor. The MC will guide the men and women to form into separate lines along the edge of the dance floor. Then the bride and groom will be invited up to the dance floor as the rest of the guests are told that this is indeed the money dance/dollar dance and they are invited to get into either of the lines."

START THE BIDDING TO KICK IT OFF ****

Ben Miller, a Wedding Entertainment Director from Illinois, suggests, "When it's time for the money dance/dollar dance, we bring the bride and groom out to the dance floor and auction off the 'coveted' opportunity to be the first to dance with them. Depending on how far our couples want to take this, we can add some humor by starting the bidding to be the first to dance with the bride at $20 and then starting the bidding for the groom at a nickel. To make it even more special, you can take a picture of the person who won the bidding and, with a small photo printer, print out a photo of the bride or groom with the person who won, put it into a frame, and give it to them at the end of the dance."

THE POLKA MONEY DANCE/DOLLAR DANCE *****

"Instead of playing the typical slow or medium-speed songs during the dance," suggests Bill Hermann, a Wedding Entertainment Director in Minneapolis, "play a series of upbeat polkas. Then, have the bride's father and groom's father regulate the lines, while exchanging the guests' larger bills for brand new one dollar bills. Instruct the guests to throw their wad of bills into the air above the bride and groom as they are sent out to cut in. Soon there will be dollar bills flying everywhere and more of your guests will not only want to participate, but they'll also bring larger bills to exchange for singles to make a larger 'cash confetti' explosion over the bride and groom than the previous person."

THE MONEY DANCE/DOLLAR DANCE
DUNK TANK *****

Bill Hermann has also offered the following suggestion for an outdoor reception. "If the bride and groom are into baseball or softball, bring in a dunk tank and get the groomsmen to volunteer to strip down to swim trunks and T-shirts. The guests will be given one ball to throw at the dunk tank for every dollar they give during the money dance/dollar dance."

WORDS OF WISDOM CARDS
INSTEAD OF CASH ****

Also from Ben Miller: "If you'd prefer not ask your guests for money, but you still want to connect with them in the manner provided by the money dance, have your guests fill out note cards with their names on one side and their best words

of wisdom for achieving a long and happy marriage. Then instead of bringing money in exchange for a dance, they will give you their words of wisdom cards and you'll have a great keepsake to take with you and read on your honeymoon."

CHAPTER 21
THE BOUQUET AND GARTER TOSS

*W*ho among your single guests will be the ones getting married next? Finding the answer to this question has been the underlying tradition and purpose of the bouquet and garter toss events for quite a long time. Nowhere are the stark differences between men and women more apparent than during these events. The single ladies, more often than not, are eager and excited to participate — not just because they may already be hoping to get married soon, but also because the thought of catching something that belonged to the bride on her wedding day is excitement enough. The single men, more often than not, come up begrudgingly and can be seen with their hands in their pockets or holding a beer, thus limiting their chances to catch the garter. On some rare occasions the gathered bachelors have been seen parting down the middle as if the garter was Moses and they were the Red Sea. The flying garter then falls towards the dance floor with nary a hand reaching out to stop its descent. In this chapter, we'll delve into some creative twists that can make these events more memorable, including some ideas that will actually make the single guys want to scramble for the flying garter!

THE TEDDY BEAR TOSS ***

Greg Lowder, a wedding entertainer in Seattle, suggests, "If you have several small children in attendance, try holding a separate toss event for the kids first. Toss a teddy bear or a large stuffed animal and take a photo with the child who catches it."

THE CANDY TOSS ***

Building on the teddy bear toss idea, Cindy Ormond, a wedding entertainer from Syracuse, New York, submitted the following idea. "Have your band or DJ play 'I Want Candy' by Bow Wow Wow or 'Sugar, Sugar' by The Archies as the young children are invited to gather on the dance floor. Then the bride and groom can dig into a sack of candy treats and start tossing them out for the children to enjoy."

THE BOUQUET PRESENTATION ✳✳✳✳

Why not do a bouquet presentation to someone you appreciate? Perhaps you might want to present it to one of your female friends who recently became engaged? Maybe you could present it to the longest married couple?

THE WISH BOUQUET ✳✳

"Invite out ALL of the ladies for the bouquet toss instead of just the single ladies," suggests Cindy Ormond. "Have your MC let them know that they should make a wish because the one who catches it will be certain to have her wish come true."

THE MIRV BOUQUET TOSS ✳✳✳

If you are worried that tossing only one bouquet will cause others to feel left out, why not toss a bouquet that breaks into four or five smaller bouquets in flight? (MIRV refers to a missile that has multiple warheads.)

INVOLVE THE MARRIED PEOPLE INSTEAD ✳✳✳✳

If you have a limited number of single friends in attendance, but still want to present your bouquet and garter to someone, try Wedding Entertainment Director Randy Bartlett's suggestion. "Bring all the married ladies up to one corner of the dance floor. Have them cross to the opposite corner (where the bride is standing) by ascending years of marriage. Upon revealing the identity of the longest married woman, have the bride present her with the toss bouquet. Repeat this process with the married men, but call them over to the groom in descending years of marriage to reveal the man who has been married the shortest amount of time. Have the groom present him with the garter."

BOUQUET AND GARTER SWITCH ***

Pull a fast one by arranging for your MC to stop the music just before the bouquet toss is about to occur. The bride will then drag the groom out and seat him in a chair as she begins pulling up his pant leg while some sexy music is playing. The guests will hoot and holler when it's revealed that the groom is wearing the garter. The bride then removes the garter and tosses it to the single ladies. Then the groom tosses the bouquet to the single men.

DON'T STOP THE DANCING ***

If the dancing is going strong and everyone is having fun, why bring it to a halt just to toss the bouquet and garter? Why not have the bride and groom do the tosses from the fully packed dance floor? The MC can instruct the single ladies and single guys to raise their hands, or you can let go of that tradition and make it fair game for anyone to catch them.

MAKE HIM DANCE FIRST ***

Before the bride will let the groom remove her garter, the MC will instruct the groom that he must put on a sexy dance for her first. Only when she finally gives him the "go ahead" wave will he at last be allowed to start removing the garter.

MAKE THE SINGLE MEN DO SOME SINGING ****

Bill Hermann, a Wedding Entertainment Director in Minneapolis, suggests, "Once the single men have been gathered, have the MC inform them that they will need to serenade the bride before the groom can remove the garter in order to show their worthiness to have a chance to catch the garter. Songs like 'My Girl' by The Temptations or 'You've Lost That Lovin' Feeling' by The Righteous Brothers can played and your MC might even lead the bachelors in a choreographed dance to the song. The singing can be stopped whenever the MC decides the timing is appropriate to move onto the groom removing garter."

SKIP THE GARTER REMOVAL ***

If you, or your guests, might be more conservative, and the removal of the garter may be perceived as too racy, just skip it. Have the groom produce the garter from a pocket. Or the bride can simply hand it to him. Then proceed with the garter toss event as you see fit.

THE BEST MAN AS A "HUMAN CHAIR" ***

Ask the best man to serve as a "human chair" for the bride to sit upon while the groom removes the garter. The best man can "get down on all fours" while the bride sits on his back, or he can get down on one knee while the bride is seated on his other leg.

THE HANDCUFFED GROOM ***

Before the garter removal begins, have the best man put the groom in handcuffs, with his hands behind his back, so he can't use his hands to remove the garter. Your entertainment vendors can play "Bad Boys" by Inner Circle (the theme for the TV show *Cops*) to really set the mood.

THE "MARY POPPINS" TRICK ***

In the movie *Mary Poppins*, the main character astounds the children in her care by pulling oversized items out of her satchel. Have the bride sit on a chair with a cloth chair cover on it. Place the chair with its back to a table covered with a tablecloth. Have an accomplice feed oversized items to the groom from under the table and the chair. One couple who suggested this idea had the groom withdraw several oversized items from underneath the bride's dress during the garter removal, including golf clubs, a carnival-sized stuffed animal, and a tall lamp. The guests could hardly contain themselves.

THE "STAR TREK" REMOVAL ***/*****

If both of you are *Star Trek* fans, have the groom enter the room wearing the classic James T. Kirk gold spandex top. Play the original *Star Trek* TV show theme while the groom lip-syncs to William Shatner's voice saying, "...to boldly go where no man has gone before!" After which the groom can take out his "tricorder" and begin taking readings while removing the garter. If your friends already know that you are both sci-fi geeks, blow their minds by proudly embracing the label.

THE "MISSION: IMPOSSIBLE" REMOVAL ***/*****

From Victoria, British Columbia, Alexander Tamas, a Wedding Entertainment Director and professional MC, says, "Why not try creating a fun, scripted introduction for the groom in the style of the TV show *Mission: Impossible*, which can be presented by the MC while the show's theme song is playing. Make something up about the garter containing a hidden microchip with information on it that could end civilization as we know it. You could even include a warning that the device is booby-trapped to go off when touched by human skin, thus requiring the groom to use his teeth."

THE SPELUNKER'S REMOVAL ***

One couple, both avid spelunkers, decided to work that interest into their garter removal in a creative way. The groom put on a head-mounted flashlight commonly used by spelunkers before proceeding to dig under the bride's dress for the elusive garter. Their friends and family got a big kick out this idea.

THE NFL GARTER TOSS ***/*****

California wedding entertainer James Loram offers another idea. "After the groom has successfully removed the garter, have the MC bring out a small football with a large marker so the bride and groom can autograph it and put their wedding date on it. While the NFL or *Monday Night Football* theme song is playing, let the groom toss the ball over the heads of the waiting bachelors. They will fight and scramble to catch the football like it's game day." If the MC can deliver a scripted narration in the style of the NFL films ("On any given Sunday…"), this event can really become five-star. This idea can be personalized in a variety of ways. The small football can be from the groom's favorite team. Or use a favorite college fight song along with a small football from that college.

OTHER SPORTS THEMES FOR THE GARTER TOSS ***/*****

Randy Bartlett of Premier Entertainment in Sacramento says, "If the groom enjoys playing golf, staple the garter to a soft golf ball and have the groom hit it to the single men with a pitching wedge. If the groom enjoys fishing, attach the garter to a fishing line and have the groom 'cast' the garter to the single guys."

One of my grooms was a big fan of Michael Jordan. Thanks to eBay, I was able to find him a signature Michael Jordan Chicago Bulls mini-basketball. His eyes lit up when I tossed him the ball so he could wrap the garter around it before tossing it to his single guy friends.

THE GARTER TOSS WITH A BRIBE ***

Use a safety pin to attach a twenty dollar bill to the garter. Play the theme song from the TV show *The Apprentice* ("For The Love Of Money" by the O'Jays) to build the energy. Watch as the single men push and shove each other as they try to catch the garter…and the cash!

JEFF & VICTORIA

MAY 30, 2004
NEWPORT BEACH, CALIFORNIA

Every Guest Was Personally Included

Jeff and Victoria wanted to create a swanky, classy reception that would still be fun and relaxing for their intimate group of friends and family. They went out of their way to make sure each and every person felt included in a personal way by designing special dedications and creative interactions to both entertain and spotlight the individuals who had played important roles in their lives.

* BOUQUET PRESENTATION

As the bouquet toss tradition goes, the young lady who catches the bride's bouquet will be the next in line to get married. In the spirit of this tradition, Victoria wanted to do something a little more personal. Instead of tossing her bouquet, Victoria chose to present it to her friend, Nancy, who was already engaged to be married.

RECEPTION AGENDA

4:00–4:40
Drinks & Appetizers

4:40
Grand Entrance
"California" by Phantom Planet

4:50
Toasts

5:00–7:00
Five-Course Dinner

5:00
1st Course — Appetizer

5:10
First Dance
"Your Song"
by Ewan McGregor

5:15
Parents Dance
"Wonderful Tonight"
by Eric Clapton

5:20
2nd Course — Soup

5:30
Longevity Spotlight

5:45
3rd Course — Salad

6:00
Jeff & Victoria's Toast

6:10
4th Course — Entrée

6:35
* Bouquet Presentation
"Someone To Watch Over Me"
by Sarah Vaughan

6:40
5th Course — Dessert

6:50
RSVP Spotlight

7:00
Cake Cutting
"Grow Old With You"
by Adam Sandler
"When I'm Sixty-Four"
by The Beatles

7:15–8:25
Open Dancing

8:25
Last Dance
"The Last Dance" by Frank Sinatra

THE GARTER AS CANNON FODDER *****

"For grooms that want to do something a bit different than the traditional garter toss," says Wedding Entertainment Director Ron Ruth of Kansas City, "I have used a confetti cannon to launch a number of garters into the air. Inexpensive garters can be purchased at a dollar store. Ten to twelve garters will suffice and they should be loaded in the cannon in advance. To be effective, however, it is important to get the bride's 'throw-away' garter in advance as well and load it into the cannon. The garter the groom removes from the bride's leg can be one of the cheaper garters. Then the cannon is presented to the groom. Once he launches the garters into the air and they have all been claimed, the single men are told that there is one garter that is different than all the others. That garter, of course, belongs to the bride. That bachelor is then invited to join the groom for a photo."

THE GARTER PLACEMENT WITH A SWITCH ****

One idea that can be highly uncomfortable for the participants is the "tradition" of having the man who caught the garter put it on the leg of the lady who caught the bouquet. (This is more commonly done at weddings on the East Coast.) However, this idea can create some good laughs if the man is blindfolded and the single lady's leg is then secretly replaced with the groom's hairy leg.

THE GARTER PLACEMENT WITH A TWIST ***

Try this garter placement idea from James Loram of Last Dance Entertainment in Fullerton, California. "Have the lady who caught the bouquet place the garter on the leg of the gentlemen who caught it. After all, he caught it; it is his garter now, isn't it? This option can create a humorous twist on an idea that can cause some feelings of awkward discomfort. Nobody feels uncomfortable for the guy having the garter placed on his leg. But watching a guy place a garter on the leg of a lady he most likely doesn't know can cause a lot of your guest to feel uneasy."

THE DATING GAME SURPRISE *****

Mark "Peace" Thomas, a Wedding Entertainment Director based in Canyon Lake, California, submitted this idea: "One of my grooms wanted to pick on his brother. As it turned out, his brother was the last person in his family who was still single. So instead of tossing the garter, the groom walked over and handed it to his brother and we immediately started playing *The Dating Game* theme music as I brought out a stool for his brother to sit on. We then set up three stools behind him for three actresses we had hired to play the parts of bachelorettes #1, #2, and #3. Their answers were pre-scripted and rehearsed and his brother couldn't stop laughing and blushing."

PICK YOUR OWN MUSIC FOR EACH MOMENT ✳✳✳

I once coached a DJ who played "You Can Leave Your Hat On" by Joe Cocker for the garter toss. Afterwards, I pointed out how that song really fit for the moment when the groom was removing the garter, but it didn't fit the introduction, when all the single men were being gathered or for the moment when they were supposed to be competing to catch the garter. Feel free to pick out at least two songs for the bouquet (intro and toss) and three or more for the garter (intro, removal, and toss). Personalizing each moment of these events musically can make them even more unique and fun.

CHAPTER 22
OTHER SPECIAL TOUCHES

*W*hen your guests attend your wedding reception, they do so because they care about you, support you, want to congratulate you, and want to celebrate with you. The most successfully entertaining receptions are the ones where your guests are invited to connect with you and each other in fun, meaningful, and memorable ways. One major reason why guests leave a reception early is because they are not enjoying themselves. If your friends and family members are overlooked during your reception, they will feel like they are only observers of your festivities. But when they are given an opportunity to connect, they will feel like highly valued contributors. After all, isn't that the reason you invited them to your wedding reception in the first place? Here's a plethora of ideas to help you build stronger connections at your celebration with the people who have already made such valuable contributions to your lives.

THE FAMILY UNITY CANDLE *****

Jim and Denise Sanchez, a wedding entertainment team from Southern California, suggested the following: "If you haven't already done a unity candle in your ceremony, consider providing for a family unity candle to be set up on your head table. Ask your MC to inform your guests about the symbolism of the family unity candle — that when your guests first arrived they were two separate families. But now that you are married, they will be celebrating together as one big happy family. The MC will then invite someone to represent both families by coming up and lighting the outer candles. This can be anyone you choose, such as your mothers, both sets of parents, or someone in your family who hasn't yet been included. The guests will then be instructed about their role. When the bride and groom make their grand entrance, and after the applause is dying down, they will take the outside lit candles and light the center candle representing the uniting of both families into one. At that moment, everyone will begin to applaud and cheer to show their support."

SIGNED, SEALED, DELIVERED ✳✳✳

At a wedding reception a few years ago, the bride forgot to bring the marriage license to the ceremony. Their officiant was a friend, in fact a very good friend. While the guests were enjoying their meal, the officiant drove back to their house and retrieved their marriage license. When he returned, we made a big show out of the best man and maid of honor signing their license as the witnesses and everyone cheered that their marriage was now "official." That was a close save for what could have been a very frustrating situation.

If your officiant is staying for your reception, you can make the signing of your marriage license into a moment that all your guests might enjoy witnessing. You could ask your band or DJ to play "Signed, Sealed, Delivered, I'm Yours" by Stevie Wonder to add even more fun to the moment. At another wedding ceremony, the bride and groom opted to have their best man and maid of honor sign their marriage license in the middle of the ceremony. At her request, we played "Sign Your Name" by Terrence Trent D'Arby in the background to add just the right touch. The guests all began to chuckle as the best man used the groom's back to sign the license.

AN EXCHANGE OF GIFTS **

Cindy Ormond, a popular wedding entertainer from Syracuse, New York, suggests, "If the two of you plan on exchanging special wedding presents to each other, consider doing this exchange in front of your guests. This lets them see another side of your relationship in a very personalized way."

MESSAGES FROM THE "BEST WISHES" HOTLINE ****

Set up a "best wishes" hotline if you have friends and loved ones who will not be able to attend your reception. Perhaps your MC or entertainment vendors will let you use their business phone line and answering machine, after business hours, so your guests who cannot attend can call in and leave their "best wishes" messages for the two of you. It would be best to let your MC edit the messages for length and impact, as you really shouldn't know the contents of these messages before they are presented. Then the best portions of these messages will be played for all the guests to hear after the toasts or towards the end of the meal. This would be a good moment to capture on video as well, so your loved ones, who participated via telephone, can see your reactions when their messages were played.

HAVE A COLORING CONTEST FOR THE KIDS ***

Randy Bartlett, a nationally known DJ trainer and Wedding Entertainment Director based out of Sacramento, California, says, "If you have several small children in attendance, bring some coloring books and a few boxes of crayons. Have your MC help them get started in a coloring contest. Don't forget to provide a small prize for all the participants."

THE CARICATURE COLORING CONTEST ***

Building on the coloring contest idea, Brandon Lindsey, a wedding entertainer in Cincinnati, Ohio, says, "Hire a caricature artist to draw the two of you dressed as the bride and groom, but ask the artist to draw you in black and white. Make photocopies of the caricature and have the children participate in a coloring contest to see who can color the two of you the best. Be prepared to have prizes for your MC to present to all of the participants."

JOHN & YVONNE

NOVEMBER 29, 2008
HUNTINGTON BEACH, CALIFORNIA

The Korean Bowing Ceremony

John and Yvonne wanted to incorporate a traditional Korean bowing ceremony in a personalized and nontraditional way. This ceremony is customarily attended by only the groom's immediate family members immediately following the wedding ceremony. Opting to make their bowing ceremony more inclusive, John and Yvonne decided to schedule theirs to take place at the conclusion of their reception. Both families, and any friends who wanted to, were invited to stay.

* DINNER

John and Yvonne met in dental school. The special favors waiting at each guest's place setting were a colorful toothbrush and a small container of dental floss. When they did a newlywed quiz later on, we had them hold up pink and blue toothbrushes to represent each other.

RECEPTION AGENDA

6:00–7:15
Drinks & Appetizers

7:15
Grand Entrance
"Touch The Sky"
by Kanye West

7:25
First Dance
"You And I"
by Michael Bublé

7:35
Family Intros & Toasts

7:55–8:50
* Dinner

8:50
Video Montage

9:00
Father/Daughter–
Mother/Son Dance
"Your Joy"
by Chrisette Michele

9:05
Longevity Dance
"Someone Like You"
by Van Morrison

9:10–9:40
Open Dancing

9:40
Bouquet & Garter Toss
"Just A Girl" by No Doubt
"Brown Eyed Girl"
by Van Morrison
"The Boys Are Back In Town"
by Thin Lizzy
"Take A Look Around"
by Limp Bizkit
"NFL Theme"
by Scott Schreer

9:50
Cake Cutting
"L-O-V-E"
by Nat King Cole
"Sugar, Sugar" by The Archies

10:10–11:00
Open Dancing

11:00
Last Dance
"Wonderful Tonight" by Eric Clapton

HAVE SOMEONE PERFORM A SONG ✱✱✱✱

If you have a musically talented friend, perhaps he or she could perform a song or two at your reception, or even for your first dance. Or maybe you, yourself, are a musician and/or a singer. Take a moment towards the end of the meal, or maybe after the cake cutting, to perform a song or two. Your new spouse will love it and your guests will certainly enjoy it as well. At a reception a few years ago in Yorba Linda, California, Mary surprised her groom, Andrew, by performing Etta James' popular ballad "At Last" after the cake cutting. Her bridesmaids helped out by serving as her backup singers and dancers. Andrew was completely surprised and the guests were blown away. Make sure to arrange with your MC ahead of time any special needs for amplifying your instruments or for securing instrumental accompaniment tracks for your performance.

SORORITY SONG FOR THE BRIDE ✱✱✱

If you, the bride, are or were a member of a college sorority, and it is traditional for your sorority sisters to serenade you with a special song at your reception, work with your MC to place it into your agenda. This event can serve as a great lead-in for the bouquet toss.

A SINGING TRIBUTE TO THE BRIDE AND/OR GROOM ✱✱✱✱

Mark "Peace" Thomas, a Wedding Entertainment Director based in Canyon Lake, California, suggests, "Have your MC ask all of the gentlemen at the reception to come up and gather in circles around the bride, with the groom and his groomsmen in the innermost circle. The MC will then lead them in a sing-along to 'My Girl' by The Temptations, with the groom and the rest of the men dropping down on one knee at the chorus. Or your MC can have all the ladies come up and circle the groom. The bride will be asked to stay next to the MC. Then the ladies are asked to congratulate the groom by singing 'My Guy' by Mary Wells and showering him with hugs and kisses on the cheek. As they wrap up the chorus, the bride finally pushes her way into the center and gives the groom a big kiss as the ladies cheer."

KARAOKE ANYONE? *****

If you and your friends are big fans of singing karaoke, perhaps you should consider bringing in a karaoke machine. The karaoke could be done in sets so your guests can also enjoy some dancing. If your guests are more likely to sing karaoke than they would be to dance, maybe opting for karaoke as the primary form of entertainment would be a better fit. Keep in mind that extra equipment will be required in addition to what a band or a DJ would normally provide, so you should expect a reasonable surcharge. Also, it would be wise to verify the skills of the person who will be your karaoke host. He should be experienced with the equipment and be skilled with keeping your guests entertained between performances. Does he have the talent to sing karaoke to get your guests warmed up?

PUT ON A CHOREOGRAPHED DANCE ROUTINE ****

One California bride came up with a creative idea that really set the mood for their open dancing. She and her bridesmaids had been rehearsing a choreographed dance routine to a song from *Grease* and were looking forward to putting on a show for the groom as a surprise. After placing this into the agenda right before the open dancing, I suggested that it might be even more fun to follow up their performance by asking the groom and his groomsmen to put on their own choreographed routine in response. Knowing her groom and his groomsmen really well, I knew they would jump at this chance. The catch was, they were not going to find out until the moment we announced it, following the ladies' show. As the bride and her bridesmaids finished their routine and the crowd was applauding, we announced that it was now the groom's turn as I handed him a hard hat and invited his groomsmen to come help out. They were completely caught off guard. But as soon as "Macho Man" by Village People began to play, they instantly began performing their own completely unrehearsed dance routine. When they finished, the crowd was cheering and giving them a standing ovation. Needless to say, getting everyone dancing was a pretty easy task after that.

At another reception, the groom was in a wheelchair, and he and his bride opted not to do a first dance. When I spoke with the bride privately, I suggested that she create a fun dance routine with her bridesmaids as a replacement for the first dance. When the time came, we sat the groom on the edge of the dance floor as his bride and her bridesmaids put on a creative routine inspired by the opening credits for the movie, *My Best Friend's Wedding*. The song they used was "Wishin' And Hopin'" by Ani Difranco. Their dance was a complete surprise for the groom and the guests, and it ended with the bride falling, as if swooning, into the groom's lap. Everyone loved it.

There are no limits to how creative you can be. Keep in mind that your guests are hoping to have an entertaining time at your reception, but when you provide some of the entertainment yourselves in an unexpected and creative way, your guests will get even more excited about helping you celebrate. Always be sure your MC knows about your plans in advance.

To see different examples of how a crowd will react to a routine like this, check out these videos posted on YouTube.com. The first link, "Wedding Party Thriller," is an homage to Michael Jackson's "Thriller" (http://www.youtube.com/watch?v=OPmYbP0F4Zw&eurl=). The second link features a completely unique routine presented by the bride's father and brothers (http://www.youtube.com/watch?v=uojhahf7lo4).

THE SLUMDOG MILLIONAIRE SURPRISE *****

Dallas/Ft. Worth-based DJ David Allen helped one of his clients develop this idea. "One of my couples wanted to create a really dramatic surprise dance. They were also big fans of the movie *Slumdog Millionaire*, which is well known for its great choreographed dance routine during the credits. After discussing our options, we decided that the best surprise would be for the bride and groom to start the dance routine when we played 'Jai Ho' from the soundtrack and then have random wedding party members, family members, and guests just start joining in without missing a step. To pull this surprise off, we secretly contacted select individuals who they knew would either be willing to participate and/or would cause quite a stir by joining in. We pointed them to a YouTube video with the choreographed moves they would need to learn before the wedding. When ten percent of the guests started participating bit by bit, following every step and move, the rest of the guests were completely caught off guard and began to cheer them on with tremendous energy."

THE MAD RUSH FOR NOISEMAKERS ***

Marcello Pedalino, a Wedding Entertainment Director from Newton, New Jersey, suggests, "For a New Year's Eve wedding, instead of handing out the noisemakers and hats around the room, put them in the center of the dance floor at 10 minutes to midnight, making it the only place in the world to be. When your MC lets the guests know to come grab them, your dance will get packed quickly and stay that way well into the New Year."

THE TOILET PAPER RACE **

Shawn Whittemore, a Wedding Entertainment Director from Lake Oswego, Oregon, submitted the following idea. "This is a silly game that makes a big mess in an effort to determine whether the bride or groom will be the one who will 'call the shots,' 'wear the pants,' or 'control the checkbook.' Your best man and maid/matron of honor are instructed to each place their index fingers into a roll of toilet paper as the bride and groom are challenged to unravel their roll the fastest. The guests will cheer them on as toilet paper goes flying everywhere."

LET'S GET READY TO RUMBLE ****

If you are both known for being overly competitive, here's another fun showdown. What are your favorite sports, pastimes, hobbies, or other competitive activities? Pick one that fits the two of you and have your MC call you out for a face-off. Some couples have challenged each other to competitions involving the video games Guitar Hero or Dance Dance Revolution. One couple chose to do a grocery-bagging competition. And one bride's favorite game was the balloon stomp. But remember, the joy of victory will always be tempered by the agony of defeat. Be sure to discuss these ideas with your MC and ask for advice on how to stage your competition.

THE NEWLYWED QUIZ *****

Texas-based wedding entertainer Andy Austin says, "Letting your guests have a good laugh at your expense can be a great way to liven things up just before kicking off the open dancing. The MC will seat the bride and groom in chairs, back to back, preferably on the dance floor, so your guests can see what's about to happen. The bride and groom will both be given objects to hold that will represent both of them, one in each hand. You can use bridal-themed Barbie and Ken dolls, small signs on a stick that have 'bride' and 'groom' (or your first names) printed on them, an empty wine bottle for the bride and an empty beer bottle for the groom, or the bride and groom can remove their shoes, and trade one apiece. The MC will then ask the bride and groom a series of pointed questions to see how well they really know each other. The questions must be precisely worded so that the only answers given are 'the bride' or 'the groom.' When questions like, 'Which one of you is the better kisser?' and 'Who is better with money?' are posed, the bride and groom will both respond candidly, without saying a word, by simply raising whichever object represents their answer. Because they are back to back, they cannot see each other's replies, which can result in some great reactions from the guests. A good MC will also be ready to ad-lib in response to any particularly funny moments as they occur."

THE NEWLYWED QUIZ WITH GUESTS' QUESTIONS *****

"Let your guests participate in the newlywed quiz by letting them submit the questions," says Jimmie Malone, a popular wedding entertainer based in Binghamton, New York. "This will cause them to be even more attentive during the quiz as they'll be waiting to see if their questions get used and looking forward to your reactions. No one knows you better than the people at your reception, so who better to help your MC develop questions that are not just read from a generic list. I'd highly recommend giving your MC permission to prescreen and edit out any questions that may not be appropriate."

IDENTIFY YOUR BRIDE ***/****

Wedding Entertainment Director Mitch Taylor from Michigan suggests, "Have your MC line up six or seven chairs on the dance floor. The MC then blindfolds the groom and fills the chairs with five or six ladies and the bride. Then the MC has the groom feel their ankles to see if he can identify his bride. Or the MC could have the lineup of ladies kiss the blindfolded groom on the cheek to see if he can identify his bride." This idea can be made even more fun by swapping out a few of the ladies with groomsmen. At one wedding, the groom was getting kisses on the cheek and when he incorrectly selected his best man as his bride, the guests all began to laugh and cheer.

THE MATCH GAME *****

Dallas-based Wedding Entertainment Director Chad Alan Wandel says, "Following the example of the '60s game show, *The Match Game*, the bride and groom can be seated in front of the head table with their wedding party members seated behind the table. The bride and groom will each be given a small dry-erase board and a dry-erase marker. Their wedding party members will be given large index cards with large Sharpie markers. The MC will read aloud a sentence with a 'blank' word missing such as

'I hate it when your mother walks in on us while we are _____ on the couch.'

Everyone writes down their answers. Then the MC will have each bridesmaid and groomsman hold up their answers for everyone to see one at a time. Then the bride and groom reveal their answers. The one with the most matches wins. This activity can be simplified by having the bride and groom separately answer questions that are put in envelopes, with the sentence to be read aloud printed on the outside of the envelope. They will be quizzed about each other's answers and whoever gets the most matches wins. This activity can take as little or as much time as you desire."

THE WEDDING PARTY SHOWDOWN *****

"Have your bridesmaids and groomsmen compete in a 'family feud' style of trivia competition," suggests Curtis Hoekstra, a Wedding Entertainment Director from Phoenix. "Your MC could go back and forth between them testing how well they know the two of you with questions like:

'What is the groom most likely to leave on the bedroom floor?' and

'What is the bride most likely to forget to bring on the honeymoon?' and

'What is the groom most likely to watch on TV?' and

'What is the bride most likely to do while driving?'

Your MC will get the correct answers ahead of time from the two of you, and your guests will enjoy watching them prove which group knows you best."

THE "LOVE STORY" PRESENTATION *****

Mark and Rebecca Ferrell, a nationally known wedding entertainment team as well as internationally recognized DJ trainers from Temecula, California, say, "Wedding receptions are a celebration of love — the love the bride and groom share for each other and the love they and their friends and family share as well. Because guests can get easily distracted, it can be common for them to lose sight of how important the reception really is for the bride and groom. After seeing guests not paying attention during the first dance at weddings, we developed the concept of the 'Love Story' as an event to keep the guests' focus and attention where it belongs during the first dance — on the bride and groom. We also found that the dramatic retelling of the story of how the couple met and fell in love made their guests feel even more connected to them both. We gather information from the bride and groom separately and then combine it into an engaging 'love story' presentation. The guests find themselves participating in the drama as we take them into humorous moments, which result in laughter, and poignantly touching moments that may draw out some emotional tears. When the story has ended and the first dance begins, all eyes will be on the bride and groom and everyone will realize just how lucky they are to have found each other. This is not just an MC reading a script. It is an emotionally moving performance piece that requires an amazing amount of talent, skill, and training to deliver effectively. When done correctly, it will be remembered for years to come. When done poorly, the results can be embarrassing and even downright painful. It is imperative to use only the very best, proven entertainer. Ask to see a video of their previous 'love story' presentations and ask about their performance background and/or training."

It should also be noted here that Mark and Rebecca Ferrell have trained talented wedding entertainers across the United States, and internationally, in performance-based workshops designed to help these entertainers present this "love story" concept as powerfully and effectively as possible. It would be well worth your time to check out the list of wedding entertainers who have been trained by Mark and Rebecca Ferrell in their love story workshops. Here is the web page that lists their workshop attendees: (http://www.MarBeccaMethod/graduates).

MATT & TENLEY

MAY 27, 2007
LAGUNA BEACH, CALIFORNIA

"Livin' On A Prayer"

Tenley shared that Matt is well known for singing Bon Jovi's "Livin' On A Prayer" whenever they were at a karaoke bar. At her suggestion, we surprised Matt after the cake cutting by handing him the cordless microphone after asking his guests if they'd like to see him sing. With his friends and family goading him on and the instrumental track of the song playing, Matt began singing his heart out.

* T-SHIRT MAN-TAGE SURPRISE

Tenley pulled off another surprise for Matt. During the open dancing, suddenly his groomsmen and a few of his other male friends were called up to the dance floor. Matt's jaw hit the floor when his friends started removing their jackets, ties, and shirts to reveal T-shirts they'd been wearing the whole day with photos of Matt growing up on their backs.

RECEPTION AGENDA

6:30–7:35
Drinks & Appetizers

7:35
Grand Entrance
"Beautiful Day"
by U2

7:45
Toasts

8:00–9:00
Dinner

9:00–9:15
The Special Dances
First Dance
"True Companion"
by Marc Cohn

Father/Daughter–
Mother/Son Dance
"Unforgettable"
by Natalie & Nat King Cole

Longevity Dance
"Let's Stay Together"
by Al Green

9:15–9:45
Open Dancing

9:45
Cake Cutting
"I Got You Babe"
by Sonny & Cher
"Jaws Theme"
by John Williams

9:55
Surprise Performance
"Livin' On A Prayer"
by Matt Lawton

10:00–11:30
Open Dancing

10:30
* T-Shirt Man-tage Surprise
"I Wanna Be Like You"
by Big Bad Voodoo Daddy

11:30
Last Dance
"Last Dance"
by Donna Summer

TELL YOUR OWN LOVE STORY *****

"While writing and practicing a love story for one of my couples," says Atlanta-based Wedding Entertainment Director Neal Howard, "I realized that no matter how I said some of the quotes, it just didn't sound right. It sounded completely unnatural. So I made up cue cards and had the bride and groom read some of their own lines. It sounded MUCH more natural coming from them."

PRERECORDED LOVE STORY
HIGHLIGHTS *****

Wedding Entertainment Director Ron Ruth shares his unique twist on the love story idea. "I engage my couples in a conversation about how they met, their first impressions of each other, how they fell in love, and how the proposal came about. With their permission, I record the entire conversation. Sometimes I even interview them apart from each other to collect some especially poignant thoughts on what they love about each other. I then cut up some of the best comments into short sound bites that can be played while I am delivering their love story presentation to add even more humorous and emotional impact."

THE VIDEO MONTAGE ***

If you decide to create a video montage to show at your reception, consider a few guidelines. A good video montage that runs too long is no longer a good video montage. One bride's father wanted to show a video he had put together that was a full hour in length. Instead, it was played during the rehearsal dinner. A good duration of a video montage is under ten minutes. If you arranged for someone to videotape your proposal, that would be great footage to include. Using a short segment of photos to honor departed loved ones will recognize their impact in your life without letting the mood come down. Formatting your video montage to play on a DVD is always better than using a laptop computer. The power supply for laptops can add noise; laptops can switch into screensaver mode unexpectedly; and laptops can sometimes be challenging to get connected with a projector. Be sure your videographer and MC run a test of the montage before the reception in case any troubleshooting is needed.

THE "INSTANT EDIT" VIDEO MONTAGE *****

If you want to make your video montage into something really remarkable, try upgrading your video package to include an "instant edit" video montage. Your guests will be amazed when they see actual live footage from your ceremony and your grand entrance included in your montage at the end of the meal. It's not easy or cheap, but the effect it will have on your guests will be amazing. To see an example of a fun "instant edit" featuring the groom and his groomsmen hamming it up, check out this video: http://www.youtube.com/tbwre#p/u/11/EePaHWfW99Y.

THE "INSTANT EDIT" PHOTO/VIDEO MONTAGE *****

Building on the "instant edit" video montage idea, Mike Colón, an internationally known wedding photographer and sought-after photography coach, says, "While your guests are enjoying their cake, why not give them (and yourselves) a sneak preview of your photo album? Using the latest in wireless technology, my assistant can begin prepping your photos just moments after I've captured them. A short montage of the best shots can then be shown set to your favorite music." I was lucky enough to see one of these "instant edit" videos with Mike's photos at a reception a few years ago. The guests loved it!

THE T-SHIRT PHOTO "MAN-TAGE" ***

One of my clients wanted to do something a little different. When we were done with the cake cutting and were about to resume the open dancing, we called the groom out to the dance floor and then invited his groomsmen and a few more of his male friends to come give him a special presentation. We played "I Wanna Be Like You" by Big Bad Voodoo Daddy as the guys all started taking off their jackets, their ties, and then their shirts. The groom was floored when they turned around to reveal that each of their T-shirts was printed on the back with a different photo of him from his growing-up years. They had been keeping this secret since well before the wedding ceremony. It seemed appropriate to call this idea the T-shirt photo "man-tage."

CHAPTER 23

THE OPEN DANCING

*I*n an AP-Brides.com poll published in June 2009, people were asked what they enjoyed most about weddings. Coming in first place, at 60 percent of the responses, was the ceremony, and following in second place (55 percent) was the music and dancing at the reception. You may find this hard to believe, but if the rest of the advice given in this book has been taken into consideration, along with the creative ideas discussed in the previous ten chapters, getting your guests to participate during the dancing won't be difficult at all. Your dance floor will be the natural destination where your guests will arrive because they will want to keep celebrating with you. If they have been having an enjoyable time, the reception has been flowing smoothly, and they've been included and engaged in the festivities from the very beginning, there will be no need for the guilt-trip tactics and the force-fed dance routines that have played such a large part in the overall negative public perceptions about wedding entertainers. However, every crowd is different. Being prepared to jump-start your open dancing (if needed) can serve as added insurance that your guests will dance. In this chapter, we'll expose some of the best-kept secrets wedding entertainers have used to kick off lively dancing in a lighthearted and engaging manner.

THE "NOT-SO-SUBLIMINAL" TIME TO START DANCING MIX ✱✱✱

Wedding Entertainer Mike Walter suggests, "A great way to get your guests ready for the start of your open dancing is to have your band or DJ play a 'not-so-subliminal' mix of songs about dancing. When the guests begin hearing this mix of songs with lyrics that talk about dancing, they will start getting mentally ready start dancing themselves. It would be advisable to start with slower energy songs and build this mix with songs that feature more and more energy in an effort to get the guests' toes tapping. Some fun suggestions for this mix can include:

'Dance Tonight' by Paul McCartney, 'Come Dancing' by The Kinks, 'Dancing In The Moonlight' by Toploader, 'Dancing On The Ceiling' by Lionel Richie, and 'Let's Dance" by David Bowie."

RESEARCH REGIONAL MUSIC SELECTIONS **

Certain songs are more popular for dancing in specific regions, not only across the United States but around the world as well. If you have a large number of guests traveling from another state or another country to attend your wedding, doing some research on the songs that are popular for dancing in their area will make them feel even more included. At one of my receptions, the groom was from New Zealand and about a third of the guests were either traveling from or were originally from New Zealand. I contacted Richard Mills, a friend of mine who is a popular wedding entertainer in New Zealand, and asked him for some ideas for dancing music that the Kiwis would enjoy. His suggestions not only worked well, but many of the guests were truly surprised to hear dance music from their homeland.

LET THE CHILDREN START THE DANCING ***

Ron Ruth, a Wedding Entertainment Director based in Kansas City, Missouri, points out, "Often a wedding reception will include a number of children that gravitate to the dance floor while the adults are finishing their meals. As the need to clear the

ANDREW & MARY

JANUARY 13, 2008
YORBA LINDA, CALIFORNIA

" *You Can't Stop The Beat* "

Andrew and Mary both shared a strong love for the musical movie *Hairspray*. They listed a few of their favorite songs from the soundtrack with their dancing requests. In between a few surprise performances, we opted to play one of their favorites, "You Can't Stop The Beat," and they began dancing and singing the song back and forth to each other.

* SURPRISE PERFORMANCE

Mary wanted to surprise Andrew after the cake cutting by singing a song for him. We seated him at one end of the dance floor and she was joined by her bridesmaids at the opposite end of the dance floor. Andrew was beaming as Mary began singing "At Last" and their guests were completely amazed.

RECEPTION AGENDA

5:30–6:55
Drinks & Appetizers

6:55
Grand Entrance
"Main Street Electrical Parade Theme"
from Disneyland

7:05
First Dance
"Ain't Misbehavin'"
by Nat King Cole

7:10
Toasts

7:30–8:30
Dinner

8:30–8:45
The Special Dances
Father/Daughter Dance
"Beauty And The Beast"
by Celine Dion
& Peabo Bryson

Mother/Son Dance
"All The Way Home"
by Andrew Peterson

Longevity Dance
"When I Fall In Love"
by Nat King Cole

8:45–9:15
Open Dancing

9:15
Cake Cutting
"Happy Together"
by The Turtles
"Everything"
by Michael Bublé

9:25
* Surprise Performance
"At Last"
by Mary with her Bridesmaids

9:45
Bouquet Toss
"Man! I Feel Like A Woman"
by Shania Twain

9:25–11:00
Open Dancing

11:00
Last Dance
"Shout"
by Otis Day & The Knights

dance floor for the special dances draws near, I have invited the parents of the little ones to participate in a dance with their children. Simple follow-along songs that are popular with small children like 'The Chicken Dance' or "The Hokey Pokey' will often do the trick. At the conclusion of the song, I simply ask the parents to take their children with them back to their seats as we are about to begin our special dances."

START OFF SLOW ***

One of the simplest methods for attracting people to an empty dance floor is to simply lower the lighting and play a well-known romantic ballad, like "Unchained Melody" by The Righteous Brothers. People dance to music they know. At a wedding reception, there will be no shortage of couples who would love to share a dance during a romantic slow song. This simple idea can also be used to recover from a dance floor that has suddenly cleared due to an undesirable music genre change (i.e. mixing from disco to current rap when the majority of the crowd may be older and not care for current rap).

THE ROMANTIC INVITATION ***

Try this idea to fill your dance floor with couples, says Minneapolis-based Wedding Entertainment Director Bill Hermann. "Ask each person, while still seated, to take the hand of the person next to him or her and quietly whisper something into their ear. After a moment, the MC will say, 'If you like what you just heard, take that person to the dance floor and reward them with a romantic dance.'"

GROUP PHOTO ON THE DANCE FLOOR ****

If your photographer is already planning to take a group photo of you with all of your guests, why not set up the shot on the dance floor just before the dancing is set to begin? Some, who might not otherwise step foot on the dance floor, will gladly come up to participate in a large group photo. Have the entertainment vendors play some upbeat music to start warming up the crowd as they are getting ready to pose. "Freeze Frame" by J. Geils Band and "Photograph" by Def Leppard are two fun songs that might fit this moment. The MC will make sure the guests can hear the photographer's instructions for the photos over the music. Then when the photos are done, the dance music will begin right away as the MC invites everyone to get involved.

THE GROUP HUG KICK OFF ****

Have your MC invite your parents to come hold hands in a tight circle around the two of you in the center of the dance floor. Next the MC will invite the wedding party to do the same in a slightly larger circle around the parents. Then invite the immediate family on the bride's side followed by the groom's immediate family to follow the pattern. Soon the out-of-town guests will be invited up followed by the local guests. Now, all of your guests will be surrounding you in concentric circles on the dance floor. There are a few different options from here. The MC could encourage the guests to squeeze into the center so they can all give you one big group hug. Once they are all packed in close, the MC will ask the bride to raise her hands so everyone can see her. At that point the MC will identify the bride as the leader and will begin a conga line song, like "Conga" by Gloria Estefan or "Hot Hot Hot" by Buster Poindexter. The MC tells the guests to grab someone else's shoulders and get in the line. If the bride makes her way through the tables and then back to the dance floor, a large portion of the guests will keep dancing from that point forward. Another direction that can be taken by the MC would be to start a few circle-oriented group songs like "New York, New York" by Frank Sinatra, "The Hokey Pokey" by Ray Anthony, or even a rendition of "The Chicken Dance." Granted, some of these songs have been truly overdone at wedding receptions, but this is your celebration. If you and your families like doing "The Hokey Pokey" or "The Chicken Dance," by all means make them a fun part of your "must play" dancing requests.

THE SHOULDER RUB/CONGA LINE ****

When it's time to get the dancing started, your MC will invite the guests to stand and place their right hip on the back of their chair. Since they have all been sitting

for awhile, they will then be asked to reach forward and massage the shoulders of the person in front of them so everyone can get nice and relaxed. Then the MC will start a conga line song, like "Conga" by Gloria Estefan or "Hot Hot Hot" by Buster Poindexter, as the guests will be told to keep their hands on the shoulders in front of them and link up with the other tables on their way to the dance floor. Soon the entire room is participating in a conga line dance that will wrap up back on the dance floor and lead into the rest of the open dancing.

THE CHICKEN DANCE/FERTILITY DANCE ****

One bride's mother had insisted that we play "The Chicken Dance" sometime during the night. After the general festivities were completed and it was time to resume the open dancing, we called the bride's father and mother to the center of the dance floor and asked the guests to form one large circle, holding hands, around the outside edge of the dance floor. Knowing that some of the guests might not have joined in if we had announced it as "The Chicken Dance," we used a ruse to get them involved instead. We shared that the bride's parents were thrilled to celebrate their daughter's wedding, but they were also hopeful that someday soon they might be able to call themselves grandparents. So, with the help of their friends and family, we told them that we were all about to do an ancient fertility dance. The guests began to groan and laugh when they heard "The Chicken Dance" begin to play, but they all danced and had fun regardless.

THE SNOWBALL DANCE ***

This dance can be used to quickly jump-start your open dancing during the wedding party dance. The MC will give instructions that when the word "snowball!" is announced, whoever is currently on the dance floor will be required to instantly go find another person to dance with among the guests who are still seated. The guests are told that they have to comply. After just a few calls of "snowball!" your dance floor will soon be packed with the majority of your guests.

THE TORPEDO DANCE *****

Bill James McElree, a wedding entertainer and bridal show producer in the Great White North of Sudbury, Ontario, says, "Building on the snowball dance idea, why not try something that is a bit more directed and engaging, known as the 'Torpedo Dance?' The MC will instruct the guests that whenever the word 'torpedo' is used, along with a physical location in the room directed by the MC, those on the dance floor will rush to the directed location and drag more dancers back with them to the dance floor. You can torpedo individual tables randomly around the room until the dance floor begins to fill. Then you can torpedo small sections of the room followed by half of the room and then the other. Soon your entire dance floor is packed and everyone is having a great time in the process."

DANCING FLASH MOB SURPRISE *****

Neal Howard, a Wedding Entertainment Director in Atlanta, shares, "At a recent wedding I discovered that most of the guests were not very enthusiastic about dancing. While the bride and groom were getting some sunset pictures taken outside, I asked the guests to help me create a fun surprise for them when they returned. On my cue, they were instructed to rush to the dance floor and start dancing. When the couple returned, I called them to the dance floor for a special dance. When I pressed 'play' on an energetic dance song, about 75 percent of the guests instantly rushed out onto the dance floor and started shakin' it up with their best dance moves. Of course, many of them stayed and continued to dance long after that song had ended. Not only did I give my bride and groom a fun surprise, but we also generated more dancing with their guests as a direct result."

THE "GOOFIEST" DANCE MOVES ***

"We have all seen it time and time again," comments Sacramento-based Wedding Entertainment Director Mike Anderson. "The crowd forms a circle to watch one person dance in the center and no one else wants to jump in and participate. This usually happens when one person outshines the rest of the group. I recommend livening up the mood by calling for him to show off his 'goofiest' dance moves. The invitation to be creative will release the anxiety of having to be a great dancer, and he can just mess around. If you see one person do something simple, ask the guest to imitate that same dance. If the guests get the hang of it, ask for the inventor's name, and name the dance after him or her. The guests will enjoy themselves and have plenty of laughs as well."

THE "JOYFUL JOYFUL" SURPRISE ★★★★

From Curtis Hoekstra, a Wedding Entertainment Director based in Phoenix, came this idea: "A recent bride and groom met in their high school's choir. After doing more research, including contacting the maid of honor before the wedding, I discovered one of their favorite group songs was 'Joyful Joyful' from the soundtrack of *Sister Act 2*. I saved the song until nearly the end of the reception to create a final boost of dancing energy. All of the bridesmaids joined around the bride, singing and dancing. It couldn't have been a bigger hit."

The example above shows how important it can be to share with your band or DJ some of the dancing songs that are favorites among your family or group of friends. When played at the right moment, these songs can really add an extra jolt of excitement and energy. The maid of honor at one of my weddings shared that the bride was a huge fan of Bon Jovi. After verifying that the bride had attended no less than ten of their concerts, I decided to pass on playing one of their more current hits and instead played one of their all-time classics, "Bad Medicine." The bride jumped up on her chair and began to sing surrounded by her bridesmaids, and the room came alive with even more energy and dancing.

"IT'S RAINING MEN" ★★★★

Wedding Entertainment Director Marcello Pedalino, from Newton, New Jersey, suggests, "Have your band or DJ give out parasols to the ladies while playing 'It's Raining Men' by The Weather Girls and then turn on the bubble machine. The MC might even lead them in a choreographed routine that involves spinning their parasols as they dance and sing together."

GREASE DANCE-OFF AND SING-ALONG ★★★★

Marcello Pedalino also suggests, "Have your wedding party members help you gather the ladies on one side of the dance floor and the guys on the other side. Ask your band or DJ to play 'Summer Nights' from *Grease* and get each side of the dance floor to sing along as the song features female voices and male voices singing back and forth to each other. Follow that song with 'Greased Lightning' and have your wedding party members lead all of the guests in a choreographed dance-off using the same moves from the scene in the movie. You can use YouTube to get the moves down in rehearsals."

Elisabeth Scott Daley, a Wedding Entertainment Director based in Williamsburg, Virginia, suggests, "As the evening is drawing to close and your guests have been enjoying dancing and perhaps drinking as well, consider mixing things up by throwing on a few 'sing-along' songs. Some suggestions include 'Don't Stop Believin' by Journey, 'American Pie' by Don McLean, 'Sweet Caroline' by Neil Diamond, and 'Piano Man' by Billy Joel. You can also use some of these songs to gather your guests into a circle as they sing with their arms around each other's shoulders while the bride and groom dance in the center. Some great suggestions can include 'Lean On Me' by Club Nouveau, 'Stand By Me' by Ben E. King, or 'New York, New York' by Frank Sinatra. For even more fun involvement, your MC could walk around the inside of the circle with a cordless handheld microphone and let some of guests sing on the mic."

Some Helpful Suggestions

1. Your band or DJ should be consulted if you want to use one of these ideas to jump-start your open dancing.

2. Make sure your MC knows that you want to do this and is fully prepared to help direct it properly.

3. You might want to request video footage from previous events so you can see how skilled your MC is when presenting these ideas.

4. Be candid with your band or DJ about your feelings on using or not using group participation dances to jump-start the open dancing.

5. Make a list of no more than fifteen "must play" dancing requests, but give your band or DJ input on all of your dance music preferences.

6. Make a list for your band or DJ of "never play" songs that you absolutely do not want played at your reception, regardless of who might request them.

7. Once your dancing requests have been clarified with your band or DJ, allow them to format the requests in whatever order their "read" of your guests leads them to do. Never dictate a set playlist and set order for your entertainment vendors. Trust their training, skill, and experience to be able to create the results you are expecting.

CHAPTER 24

THE LAST DANCE

*A*ll good things must eventually come to an end. The same is true for every great reception celebration. The big question is, will your ending be forgettable or unforgettable? Will your guests leave with glowing comments of praise, raving about the enjoyable time that was had by all? Will they filter out little by little as the party goes later and later into the night? Will the majority of them join you for one last dance before you head off to your honeymoon? Will your last dance be a fast-paced song that holds special memories for you and your small group of college friends that have stayed until the very end? There is no wrong or right answer to any of these questions. Only you can determine what kind of ending will best fit your wedding reception celebration. Let's go over a few options for making your last dance bring closure to your party in a truly memorable way.

LEAVE THEM WANTING JUST A LITTLE MORE ****

When your reception comes to a close, if your guests say "boo" or start chanting "one more song," it's a pretty safe bet that your entertainment vendors have done a tremendous job. There is a reason why most movies don't go longer than two hours. The same can be said for most concerts. Knowing "when to say when" is one of the most important aspects of creating good entertainment. If you choose to end your reception a little earlier than originally planned because you want to end things on a high note (and perhaps you are both getting worn out), you will be joined during your last dance by a larger percentage of your guests and your ending will be truly memorable for all. One couple at a Sunday evening wedding told me they were pretty sure their guests would not dance at their reception. After I got the entire group dancing to about five songs in a row, they asked to begin the last dance an hour earlier than their location required the party to end. They opted for the early ending because they wanted to end on a high note, and they couldn't imagine anything topping the unexpected, yet energetic dancing.

DO AN ENCORE ★★★★

Just like a memorable concert, the last song is not always the last song. Many bands will come back out as the crowd is still cheering and play an encore. You can create the same effect for your last dance. Select a slow song for your band or DJ to play and have it announced as the last dance. When the song concludes, following your prior instructions, the MC will ask your guests if they'd like one more song. If the dancing has been fairly energetic, the crowd will most assuredly respond with a resounding "yes!" Then your band or DJ can fulfill their demands by playing one last fast song that they have been saving just for the encore.

THE CIRCLE OF LOVE ★★★/★★★★★

Have the MC invite everyone to make a big circle around both of you during your last dance. Getting everyone involved in this moment not only makes it more memorable, but it can also result in some fantastic photos of the two of you surrounded by all your friends and family in the closing moments. Your MC may have some special methods for making this into a five-star event, but don't spoil the surprise by asking.

"BEST WISHES" FROM THE CIRCLE OF LOVE ****

Building on the "Circle of Love" idea, Randy Bartlett, a nationally known DJ trainer and Wedding Entertainment Director in Sacramento, says, "Have your MC move quickly around the circle of guests during your last dance, letting each of them express their best wishes to both of you on the microphone. Your MC will most likely need an assistant to keep the music running."

SAY YOUR "GOODBYES" FROM THE CIRCLE OF LOVE ****

Move around the circle bidding farewell and expressing your appreciation to each person who has remained until the end of your reception. Depending on the size of your group, you may want to select more than one song for this last dance.

INVITE YOUR GUESTS TO MAKE A BIG MESS! ****

Dallas wedding entertainer Andy Austin suggests, "Have your MC hand your guests confetti sticks and streamers that can be used during your last dance to create an ending that looks like a paper factory just exploded! Just make sure to clear this idea in advance with the staff at your location."

Dance… Eat… Dance… Eat… Dance

Michael and Lisa knew that their guests were familiar with the usual West Coast format where the dancing only starts after the meal has ended. However, they had been guests at a reception with the East Coast format that features dancing between each of the courses, and they had enjoyed it so much, they insisted on creating the same format for their reception. With a simple explanation to their guests about how their evening would be filled with dancing and eating, their guests were thrilled to help make it happen.

* LAST DANCE

Michael and Lisa chose a great last dance song. When their guests began forming a large circle around them on the dance floor, it only got better when they were all pointing at the two of them and singing, "Don't Stop Believin'!"

RECEPTION AGENDA

5:00–6:20
Drinks & Appetizers

6:20
Grand Entrance
*"You Shook Me
All Night Long"
by AC/DC*

6:30
First Dance
*"(Everything I Do)
I Do It For You"
by Bryan Adams*

6:35–6:50
Open Dancing

6:50
Fathers' Toasts

7:00–7:25
Salad Course

7:25
Formal Toasts

7:30–7:50
Open Dancing

7:50–8:30
Entrée Course

8:30
**Father/Daughter-
Mother/Son Dance**
*"Unforgettable"
by Natalie & Nat King Cole*

8:35–9:15
Open Dancing

9:15
Cake Cutting
*"Grow Old With You"
by Adam Sandler*

*"I'm Yours"
by Jason Mraz*

9:30–11:00
Open Dancing

11:00
* Last Dance
*"Don't Stop Believin'"
by Journey*

CHAPTER 25

THE BIG SENDOFF

*W*hen your last dance has ended, you can say goodbye to your guests, one at a time, or you can wave to all of them at the same time as they give you a sendoff to remember. When and how you do your last dance is primarily about providing closure for your guests. Having a big sendoff will help to solidify those feelings, but more importantly, it will also serve as the final chapter of your own memories. Do you want the final mental images of your reception to be of loading up your presents and watching as your decorations are taken down? Or would you like to run to your waiting limousine as your guests cheer your departure? In this chapter, we'll wrap up with a few unique ways to exit your celebration that will be simply unforgettable.

THE HUMAN TUNNEL EXIT ***

If your options for a memorable exit are limited, or you just want keep things simple, have your MC instruct your guests to form two lines facing each other, starting from the exit doors back to the dance floor. When the guests are all in position, they'll be instructed to raise their arms over the opening between them, forming a human tunnel. Then you will both race though the tunnel as your guests cheer your departure.

THE PETAL TOSS EXIT ***

Have the catering staff or your coordinator provide your guests with paper cones filled with flower petals as they head outside to prepare for your exit. The MC will keep you inside until everyone is in position. Then the two of you will race outside as the guests shower you with flower petals and adulation.

THE BUBBLES EXIT ***

Have the catering staff or your coordinator provide your guests with mini bottles of bubbles as they head outside to prepare for your exit. The MC will keep you

inside until everyone is in position and the bubbles have filled a large enough volume of space for your dramatic exit. Then the two of you race outside and dash through a cloud of bubbles on your way to your transportation.

THE SPARKLER EXIT ***

Have the catering staff or your coordinator provide your guests with sparklers and lighters as they head outside for your exit. The MC will keep you inside until everyone is in position and their sparklers are all lit. The two of you then race outside as the guests begin to cheer and wave their sparklers in the air. (Always check this out with your reception location in advance due to possible fire hazard issues. And it's always wise to test your sparklers before buying a large quantity, to see which ones will last the longest and give off the least amount of smoke.) To speed up lighting the sparkler, consider placing a few large lit candles in metal coffee cans along the exit path. Fill the coffee cans around the candles with sand so your guests can quickly extinguish and dispose of the sparklers safely after your exit.

THE PAPARAZZI EXIT ***

The guests are given disposable cameras as they head outside to prepare for your exit. Have the MC encourage those with their own flash cameras to bring them outside as well. When everyone is in position, the two of you race outside as the guests greet you like a rabid throng of paparazzi trying to capture photos of a Hollywood's latest power couple arriving for a movie premiere.

THE STAR WARS SENDOFF ★★★★

For *Star Wars* fans, Matt Graumann, a Wedding Entertainment Director in Simi Valley, California, says, "Have your guests line up outside on either side of the pathway for your exit. Pass out lighted toy light sabers and play 'Throne Room and Finale' by John Williams from the soundtrack of *Star Wars: Episode IV* as you make your grand exit."

THE HAND-DRAWN CARRIAGE EXIT ★★★★★

Kevin Cordova, a popular wedding entertainer in Las Vegas, builds on the hand-drawn carriage entrance idea from Chapter 15. "Find a white, hand-drawn carriage and enlist two ushers or groomsmen to bring it to the center of the dance floor following the last dance. The guests can be instructed to form a gauntlet inside the room leading to the exit or outside leading to your departure vehicle. When the guests are in place, the bride and groom will get into the carriage and give their best parade waves to their guests as they make their dramatic exit."

Some Helpful Suggestions

1: Your location should be consulted if you want to create a big sendoff. There may be local noise ordinances that prohibit them.

2: This would be a great moment to capture on film or video. However, if your photographer or videographer has already departed, consider arranging for someone else to take some photos and/or video footage of your exit.

3: Make sure your MC knows that you want to do this and is fully prepared to help direct it properly.

4: You may want to change into your departure outfits before your exit, or you may prefer to leave in your wedding attire. Either way, make arrangements to have someone pack your bags in your transportation for you before making this dramatic exit.

NICK & SOPHIE

JANUARY 10, 2010
FULLERTON, CALIFORNIA

"Light 'Em Up"

Following their last dance, Nick and Sophie's guests were asked to help give them a sendoff they wouldn't soon forget. With some fast-paced music playing to create a sense of urgency, their guests all quickly went outside and lined up on either side of the walkway leading to the limo that was waiting to whisk the bride and groom away. Each guest was provided with sparklers. Once all of the sparklers were lit, Nick and Sophie made their departure while their friends and family cheered them on their way.

* FIRST DANCE WITH VIDEO MONTAGE

While Nick and Sophie were sharing their first dance together as husband and wife, their guests were treated to a breathtaking video montage featuring photos of the two of them growing up, with their friends, and highlights from their relationship. The images were displayed on four large screens mounted in faux picture frames hanging on either side of their ballroom.

RECEPTION AGENDA

5:00–6:00
Drinks & Appetizers

6:00
Grand Entrance
"Beautiful Day" by U2

6:10
Toasts

6:25-7:20
Dinner

7:20-7:35
The Special Dances
*** First Dance
with Video Montage**
*"We Will Dance"
by Steven Curtis Chapman*

Father/Daughter Dance
"Joy" by George Winston

Mother/Son Dance
*"You Raise Me Up"
by Josh Groban*

Longevity Dance
*"Young At Heart"
by Frank Sinatra*

7:35-8:00
Open Dancing

8:00
Cake Cutting
*"How Sweet It Is
(To Be Loved By You)"
by Michael Bublé
"Recipe For Love"
by Harry Connick, Jr.*

8:10
Money Dance

8:25
Bouquet & Garter Toss
*"Single Ladies (Put A Ring On It)"
by Beyoncé
"The Boys Are Back In Town"
by Thin Lizzy
"Mission: Impossible Theme"
by Adam Clayton & Larry Mullen
"NFL Theme"
by Scott Schreer*

8:35-8:55
Open Dancing

8:55
Last Dance
*"New York, New York"
by Frank Sinatra*

THE HAWAIIAN SENDOFF *****

Wedding Entertainment Director Ron Ruth, based in Kansas City, Missouri, shares this story: "I recently had a best man, who was the groom's brother, contact me before a wedding reception to discuss a special sendoff for the bride and groom. Because they were planning to spend their honeymoon in Hawaii, we decided to enlist the help of the entire wedding party. As the reception came to a close, we seated the bride and groom on chairs in the center of the dance floor. I then told the guests that the bride and groom were leaving the following morning for a honeymoon in Hawaii and that the groom's brother and wedding party wanted to offer them a very special 'aloha.' At that moment, the best man and the groomsmen entered from the hallway wearing hula skirts over their tux pants. They had removed their shoes and socks and had rolled up the legs of their slacks. The bridesmaids followed, each with an arm full of leis. As soon as the gentlemen had lined up in front of the bride and groom, I played Elvis Presley's 'Hawaiian Sunset' as they comically wiggled their hips like hula dancers. While they were dancing, the bridesmaids placed leis on each guest and handed them each an extra one to place on the bride and groom. The laughter and fun exceeded even my expectations as the groomsmen pulled the groom from his chair and placed a grass skirt on him, insisting he join in the hula dancing."

THE SURPRISE RUNNING EXIT ****

Sacramento-based Randy Bartlett, a Wedding Entertainment Director, says, "Work with your MC ahead of time to prepare a surprise for your guests that will take place right after your last dance has finished. When the song ends, your MC will ask (over the microphone) where the two of you are going on your honeymoon. As soon as you shout back your answer, you both make a mad dash for the exit! This can be a great idea if you have a flight to catch and really do need to make a fast getaway. Just be sure your goodbyes have been completed before your last dance begins."

THE EARLY ENDING INTO THE SURPRISE "AFTER PARTY" ****

Randy Bartlett also offers this suggestion: "Combine a memorable ending with an extended evening of dancing by staging an 'early ending' with a finale song (including a send-off if you'd like). Then have your MC announce the beginning of 'the after party' where the music can be geared more towards the younger guests who will be more likely to stay later into the night. This will give the older guests, who might be inclined to leave early, the feeling that they have participated in the entire reception."

Additional Resources

Because new music is always coming out, I decided to avoid including dated music lists in this book. However, lists of suggestions for background music, ceremony music, reception events music, and dancing requests can be received for FREE by registering on the resources section of this book's Web site. Additional FREE materials including forms, video links, and articles can be accessed there as well. You can register at the following link: http://www. TheBestWeddingReceptionEver.com/Resources/Resources.html

Credits and Sources

PHOTO CREDITS

I will remain eternally grateful for the amazing images provided by the following photographers, along with my former clients and their friends and family members who have graciously allowed me the privilege of using their photographs. Foremost among them has been the staff of Jim Kennedy Photography. The contents listed here can also be found with active hyperlinks on the Photo Credits page of the book's Web site. Just visit: http://www.TheBestWeddingReceptionEver.com/PhotoCredits/PhotoCredits.html.

Jim Kennedy, Stephanie Brockman-Kennedy, Amanda Collins, and Eric Cotter

Jim Kennedy Photographers
http://www.JimKennedyPhotographers.com
They provided all of the photos on the front and back cover along with Peter Merry's portrait.
Pages: 13, 15, 27, 31, 94, 95, 99, 103, 123, 131, 140, 142, 149, 151, 155, 173, 177, 187, 211, 214, 216, 220, 227, 231

(Alphabetical by Last Name)

Jade Alayne
Jade Alayne Photographer
http://www.WeddingsByJade.com
Pages: 82, 84, 165

Joel Austell
Joel Austell Photographer
http://www.JoelAustell.com
Pages: 57, 91, 195, 226

Jared Bauman
Bauman Photographers
http://www.BaumanWeddings.com
Page: 25

Jen Bosma
Jen Bosma Photography
http://www.JBosma.com
Pages: 105, 115, 163

Jason Boulanger
Harvard Photography
http://www.HarvardPhotography.com
Page: 58

Mark Brooke
Mark Brooke Photographers
http://www.MarkBrooke.com
Page: 61

Nicole Caldwell
Nicole Caldwell Photography
http://www.NicoleCaldwell.com
Page: 197

Mike Colón
Mike Colón Photography
http://www.MikeColon.com
Pages: 54, 85, 116

Megan Cox
Timeless Ranch Photography
http://www.TimelessRanchPhotography.com
Page: 41

Michael Erdkamp
Memories by Michael Photography
http://www.MemoriesByMichael.com
Pages: 92, 154, 160, 192, 219

Stephanie Fay
Stephanie Fay Photography
http://www.StephanieFay.com
Page: 139

Tony Florez
Tony Florez Photography
http://www.TonyFlorez.com
Pages: 50, 166, 181

Mike Gillmore
Mike Gillmore Photography
http://www.MikeGillmorePhotography.com
Pages: 8, 20, 62, 76, 132, 175, 196, 199, 201

Chris Humphreys
Chris Humphreys Photography
http://www.ChrisHumphreys.com
Pages: 28, 112, 159, 180, 217

Pat Jarrett
Digital Love
http://www.ThisIsDigitalLove.com
Page: 23

Taek Jun
Taek Photography
http://www.TaekPhoto.com
Page: 203

Dave Kotinsky
Dave Kotinsky Photography
http://www.DaveKotinsky.com
Pages: 129, 225

Jeffrey Neal Lawler
Jeffrey Neal Photography
http://www.JNPStudios.com
Pages: 89, 97, 138, 144, 147, 178, 190, 204, 212, 232

Ira Lippke
Ira Lippke Studios
http://www.IraLippke.com
Pages: 44, 68, 98, 119, 124, 126, 156, 209, 229

Matthew Morgan
Matthew Morgan Photography
http://www.Matthew-Morgan.com
Pages: 40, 127

Bob Ortiz
Ortiz Photography
http://www.BobOrtiz.com
Page: 183

Prasad
Prasad Photography
http://www.PrasadPhoto.com
Page: 172

Garrett Ritchea
Garrett Michael Photography
http://www.GarrettMichael.com
Pages: 65, 117, 176

Mark Romine
Mark Romine Photography
http://www.RomineWeddings.com
Page: 184

Victor Sizemore
Victor Sizmore Photography
http://www.VCSPhoto.com
Page: 52

Bob Stambach
Bob Stambach Photography
http://www.BobStambachPhotography.com
Pages: 111, 161

Leslie Wandel
Studio W Photography
http://www.StudioWPhotography.com
Pages: 34, 35

Julie Weaver
Julie Weaver Photography
http://www.JulieWeaverPhotography.com
Page: 136

Page 45 features room layout diagrams designed by the author.

Page 70 features 3 anonymous photo submissions of DJ set-ups, and 2 which were submitted with permission by the owners. From top to bottom: **Photo 1** was submitted anonymously, **Photo 2** was submitted anonymously, **Photo 3** was submitted anonymously, **Photo 4** was submitted by Bob Carpenter of Main Event Weddings in Greenville, RI. To contact Bob Carpenter for more information, please visit his Web site: http://www. MainEventWeddings.com. For more information on the BOSE L1 Cylindrical Radiator System, visit the BOSE Web site: http://www.BOSE.com/controller?event=VIEW_STATIC_PAGE_EVENT&url=/shop_online/speakers/portable_ amplification_systems/index.jsp. **Photo 5** was submitted by Andy Austin of Andy Austin Entertainment in Dallas, TX. To contact Andy Austin for more information, please visit his Web site: http://www.AndyAustin.com.

CREATIVE IDEA CREDITS

This book contains dozens of creative ideas for creating uniquely personalized memorable moments at a wedding reception. Many of the ideas included were graciously submitted by associates of mine who deserve to be credited for their contributions. The contents listed here can also be found with active hyperlinks on the Idea Credits page of the book's Web site. Just visit: http://www.TheBestWeddingReceptionEver.com/IdeaCredits/IdeaCredits.html.

(Alphabetical by Last Name)

David Allen
Cassidy's Entertainment
http://www.DJDavidAllen.com

Mike Anderson, WED
Mike Anderson Weddings
http://www.MikeAndersonWeddings.com

Randy Bartlett, WED
Premier Entertainment & Video
http://www.PremierEntertainment.biz

Mike Colón
Mike Colón Photography
http://www.MikeColon.com

Elisabeth Scott Daley, WED
Liz Daley Events
http://www.LizDaleyEvents.com

Scott Faver
The Party Favers
http://www.ThePartyFavers.com

Matt Graumann, WED
Matt Graumann Entertainment
http://www.MattGraumann.com

Curtis Hoekstra, WED
Remarkable Receptions
http://www.RemarkableReceptions.com

Doug LaVine, WED
Music on the Move DJs & MCs
http://www.MusicOnTheMoveDJs.com

Greg Lowder
Affairs to Remember Entertainment
http://www.DJSeattle.com

Mike Anderson, WED
Creative Memories Entertainment
http://www.CreativeMemoriesDJ.com

Andy Austin
Andy Austin Entertainment
http://www.AndyAustin.com

Jim Cerone, WED
Jim Cerone, Inc.
http://www.JimCerone.com

Kevin Cordova
DJs To You
http://www.DJsToYou.com

Bettie-Jeanne Rivard-Darby
DreamView Productions
http://www.DreamViewProductions.com

Mark & Rebecca Ferrell
MarBecca Method
http://www.MarBeccaMethod.com

Bill Hermann, WED
Bill Hermann Entertainment
http://www.BillHermann.com

Neal Howard, WED
Atlanta's Best DJ
http://www.AtlantasBestDJ.com

James Loram
Last Dance Entertainment
http://www.LastDance.net

Jimmie Malone
Exceptional Receptions
http://www.ExceptionalReceptions.com

Bill James McElree
Absolute Entertainment
http://www.SudburyBride.com

Cindy Ormond
Ormond Entertainment
http://www.OrmondEntertainment.com

Ron Ruth, WED
Ron Ruth Weddings
http://www.RonRuthWeddings.com

Jay Sims, WED
Something 2 Dance 2
http://www.Something2Dance2.com

Mitch Taylor, WED
Taylored Weddings
http://www.TayloredWeddings.com

Mike Walter
Elite Entertainment
http://www.EliteEntertainment.com

Shawn Whittemore, WED
Event Team Entertainment
http://www.EventTeamEnt.com

Ben Miller, WED
Premier Productions
http://www.ThePremierProductions.com

Marcello Pedalino, WED
MMP Entertainment
http://www.MMPEntertainment.com

Jim & Denise Sanchez
Audio Cat Entertainment
http://www.AudioCatEntertainment.com

Alex Tamas, WED
Alexander's Music Service
http://www.AlexandersMusicService.com

Mark "Peace" Thomas, WED
Awesome Entertainment
http://www.Awesome-Entertainment.com

Chad Alan Wandel, WED
Chad Alan Events
http://www.ChadAlanEvents.com

Larry Williams, WED
Remarkable Weddings
http://www.RemWed.com

SOURCES

Also included here is further source information on the studies cited within this book. The contents listed here can also be found on the resources section of the Web site for the book, with active hyperlinks that can be accessed for FREE by registering. Just visit: http://www.TheBestWeddingReceptionEver.com/Resources/Resources.html.

page 28: DiscJockeyAmerica.com poll survey results. (Actual figure 85.5 percent) Retrieved October 5, 2004, from DiscJockeyAmerica.com Web site

page 29: *St. Louis Bride & Groom Magazine* of July 2003, page 106

page 30: Mark Ferrell from his "Getting What You're Worth" Seminar. Presented at the Mobile Beat DJ Show on February 22, 2000. Mark Ferrell can be contacted for more information via his Web site: http://www.MarBeccaMethod.com "Getting What You're Worth" on CD can be purchased from Mark Ferrell on his Web site: http://www.MarBeccaMethod.com/products-page/cds-and-dvds/getting-what-youre-worth/

page 72: "The do-it-yourself wedding soundtrack" by Angel Rozas. Published in the *Chicago Tribune* on August 13, 2006. A copy of the article can be seen here: http://www.TheBestWeddingReceptionEver.com\Resources\Soundtrack\Soundtrack.html

page 150: Tom Haibeck is the author of *Wedding Toasts Made Easy* and *The Wedding MC*. Tom Haibeck can be contacted for more information via his web site: http://www.WeddingToasts.com

page 215: "The AP-Brides.com POLL" conducted by GfK Roper Public Affairs & Media. Published on AP-Gfk Poll Web site June 1, 2009. http://www.ap-gfkpoll.com/pdf/AP-GfK_Brides.com_Topline.pdf

Submit Your Wedding Idea

If you have a creative wedding entertainment idea, or a story of a uniquely entertaining moment that occurred at a wedding reception, please feel free to send in any submissions to be considered for future editions of this book. All submissions will be given consideration and any the author selects to include in future editions of the book will be credited and referenced in this credits and sources section with a Web site address, e-mail, or other preferred contact information. Please e-mail all submissions to: FunIdeas@TheBestWeddingReceptionEver.com

Acknowledgments

There are so many people to thank for inspiring me, encouraging me, and supporting me, but I want to start off by thanking God for creating me and giving me the talents and gifts that have enabled me to provide for my family through my wedding entertainment services.

Next, I want to thank my wife, Lisa, for her tireless support and never-ending belief that this book could actually be completed someday. I'd also like to thank Rick Warren for starting Saddleback Church all those years ago so I could find a church family right when I needed one most. I want to thank Mark and Rebecca Ferrell for sharing their insights with me, for opening doors for me, and for telling me I could do it, even when everyone else said it wasn't possible to make a living as a wedding entertainer. Thanks to Randy Bartlett for helping me to stay on task and for representing everything that is truly good about being a professional wedding entertainer. I'd like to thank Jim Kennedy for his generosity with the amazing photos featured on the cover and throughout this book. I'd like to thank Brian and Jennifer Varca for allowing me to use their wedding photos on the cover and inside my book. A special thank-you also goes out to all of the other talented photographers and wedding clients who have graciously allowed me to use their images inside my book. (They are all listed in the Credits and Sources section.) And I'd also like to thank James Loram for not only being a great business partner with my previous entertainment service, Last Dance Entertainment, but also for just being a great friend.

I will be forever grateful to Megan Hiller, senior editor with Sellers Publishing, for believing in this book and for helping me take it "pro." Many thanks as well to the entire staff at Sellers Publishing, from the copy editors and the graphic designers to the sales and marketing team.

For her invaluable help as my first official editor, I'd like to thank Amanda Jerome. For their additional editing help, I'd also like to thank my good friends, Ron Ruth, Melissa Churchwell, Steve Otto, Alex Tamas, Amy Hoekstra, David Miller, and Elisabeth Scott Daley.

Thank you, Tom Haibeck, for contributing such a thoughtful foreword and for your generous help with getting my first, self-published version of this book printed and promoted.

I owe a considerable amount to each of the entertainers who generously shared their ideas with me so I could, in turn, share them with my readers. (They are all listed in the Credits and Sources section.) The most generous of all have been the charter members of the Wedding Entertainment Directors Guild (W.E.D.Guild), who have proven themselves to be among the most talented wedding entertainers around. They are certainly worthy of being the first to wear the prestigious title of Wedding Entertainment Director. Listed in alphabetical order, they are: Mike Anderson (of CA), Mike Anderson (of MN), Randy Bartlett, Jim Cerone, Elisabeth Scott Daley, Matt Graumann, Bill Hermann, Curtis Hoekstra, Neal Howard, Doug LaVine, Ben Miller, Marcello Pedalino, Ron Ruth, Jay Sims, Alex Tamas, Mitch Taylor, Mark "Peace" Thomas, Shawn Whittemore, Chad Wandel, and Larry Williams.

There are countless entertainers, organizations, and groups in my professional world to thank. Here are just a few of them:

My Advisory Board of Directors with the W.E.D.Guild, the ADJA National Board of Directors, my fellow ADJA members, my local Southern California ADJA Chapter members, everyone at DiscJockeyAmerica.com, my former podcast listeners at DJARadio.com, Ryan Burger and his staff at Mobile Beat Magazine & Shows, including Mike Buonaccorso and Bob Lindquist, John Young and his staff at the Disc Jockey News & Conferences, Dennis Hampson and Dave Hastings with the CPDJA.

The members of TT, MAPDJ, GHAMMA ABC, NACE, NAWP, ISES, WMBA, WPIC, and AFWPI.

David Allen, Daren Anderson, Andy Austin, Tony Barthel, Austin Beaver, Cliff Bell, Nelson Bennett, Ray Bernal, Matt Bixby, Ryan Bombard, Marc Brooks, Craig Brown, David Browne, David Browning, Jon Bruce, Kelli Burns, KC Campbell, Peter Carroll, Albin Castillo, Stuart Chisholm, Mike Connolly, Michael Coombs, Chris Costa, Alvis Darroch, Jim Darby, Bettie-Jeanne Rivard-Darby, Ken Day, Jason Diavatis, Wayne Dickson, Chad Dowling, Dr. Drax, Patrick Durham, Darryl Elkins, Tommy & Cindy Evans, Gary Fernandez, Howard & Leslie Fisher, Bryan Foley, Ed Frank, Richard Frohman, James Gammell, Roderick Gaerlan, Adele Georgetti, Yogi Goyal, Danny Goyer, Brian Graham, Dean Hall, Monica Hamblin, John Hanrahan, Roy Hanschke, Doug & Dara Harmon, Paul Harms, Brian Harris, Kemp Harshman, Lee Haynes, Jose Heredia, Eric Herod, Steve Hoffman, Bob Holl, Jim Horn, Eric Hovey, John Howard, Tim Howard, Robert Huggins, George James, Joel-Steven, Michael Johnson, Lisa Kasberg, Rodger Kauffmann, Don Kilbury, Paris Kiriakis, Tim Knapton, George Koury, Charles LaMantia, Gary Lankford, Marc Lanning, Garrett LaPratt, Jack Lillian, Brandon Lindsey, Randy Lira, Mike Lonneman, Albert Lopez, David Louis, Ed Lovato, Bill Lovelace, Greg Lowder, Jimmie Malone, Joe Martin (of AZ), Joe Martin (of MO), Joe Martin (of TX), Matt Martindale, Jody & Tammy Maxx, Bill James McElree, Neal McKinney, Peter Merkle, Ron Michaels, Lisa Miller, Richard Mills, Matt & Tamara Mitchell, Derrick Munoz, David Nazario, Wade Nelson, Jonathan Novich, Vicki Orgill, Cindy Ormond, Gabriel Ortiz, Manny Otero, Steve Otto, Phil Peralta, Francisco Perez, Michael Peterson, Daniel Pizano, Robert & Stephanie Poff, Dodie Rahlmann, Martin Ramirez, Anthony Rice, Jake Ritchie, Jim & Denise Sanchez, Shawn & Erica Schiller, Steve Sharp, Tamara Sims, Brian Smith, David Smith, Rob Snyder, Gil Sotelo, Alvin Sowers, Jason Spencer, Doug Stanley, Michael Stedman, Randal Stout, Hugh Swanke, David Tanksley, Jerry Taylor, Scott Topper, Wade VanDerBoom, Chris Vito, Jeffrey Weil, Rick Whitehead, Shawn Willms, Roger Yager, Scott Yoffe, Donnie Zahand, Chris Allison, Joe Balice, Jeff Blugrind, Cap Capello, Jim Casey, Tom Catucci, John Christian, Chris Curto, Karl Detken, Brian Doyle, Richard Duffie, Andy Ebon, Aaron Fox, Tom French, John Gallagher, Scott Goennier, Ken Heath, Jeff Hooten, Mark Hudnall, Craig Johnson, Jason Jones, Ron Jones, Brett Khan, Danette Koharchik, Greg "DJ Chopper" Lammers, Al Lampkin, Allen Layton, Dave Lewis, Nick Logan, Michael McCune, Scott McDonald, Alan & Debbie McKenzie, Chris Meschuck, Joseph Mire, Todd Mitchem, Stephen Moore, Calvin Morgan, Eric Moss, Derrick Munoz, Todd Powers, Kenny Quinterro, Toby Rechenamacher, Corey Rock, Orlando Rodriguez, Scott Siewert, Adam Skuba, Bill Smith, Terry Smith, Ty & Mari Smith, Xanthin Smith, Adam Sokool, Olyn Taylor, Mike Vaillencourt, David Van Enger, Timmy Vanderbilt, Mark Wakelin, Andrew Walker, Dude Walker, Dan Walsh, Robert Arthur, Cesar Cosio, Jeffrey Craig, Tom Daddazio, Bob Deyoe, Scott Faver, Tara Feely, "Sonny" Gallardo, Miles Gilbert, Jeffrey Greene, Joe Hecht, Johnny Kelly, Mark Klatskin, KC KoKoruz, Bob Kramarik, Marz & Amy Lawhorn, Jorge Lopez, Edwin McMurty, Joe Murphy, Dan Ohrman, Randi Rae, Rod Randall & Renee Retherford, John Rozz, J.R. Silva, Gerry Siracusa, Pete Troy, Mike Walter, Adam Weitz, Russ Welch, George Whitehouse, Bill Willets, Jade Alayne, Joel Austell, Jared Bauman, Jen Bosma, Mark Brooke, Nicole Caldwell, Mike Colón, Megan Cox, Aaron & Jenn Delesie, Michael Erdkamp, Stephanie Fay, Tony Florez, Mike Gillmore, Chris Humphreys, Pat Jarrett, Taek Jun, Jim Kennedy, Dave Kotinsky, Jeffrey Neal Lawler, Ira Lippke, Matthew Morgan, Bob Ortiz, Nrapendra Prasad, Garrett Ritchea, Mark Romine, Bob Stambach, Victor Sizemore, Leslie Wandel, Julie Weaver, Carl Young, Heather Howery, Rev. Clint Hufft, Will Hegarty, Shannon Underwood, and Ira Gold.

On a personal note, special thanks are due to: my stepsons, Eric and Jason Lovato; my family in Seattle including my brother Jesse, my sister-in-law Ramara, my nephews, Russell and James, my mother, Donna, my father, Pete, and the rest of the Merrys and Browns. This book is also dedicated to the memory of "my buddy" Carl Kudell. "Sweet!" will always be my favorite first review.

And finally, I'd like to thank each and every couple who ever trusted me with their wedding entertainment. This book has only been made possible because you believed in me enough to keep me in business all this time.